AF585501

WHEN WORDS FAIL US

STAN GRANT is a proud Wiradjuri man, and the Vice Chancellor's Chair of Australian-Indigenous Belonging at Charles Sturt University. He was formerly ABC's Global Affairs and Indigenous Affairs Analyst. He is the award-winning and bestselling author of several books, including *Talking To My Country*, *The Queen Is Dead*, *Murriyang* and *Australia Day*.

WHEN WORDS FAIL US

TRUTH BEYOND TIME

STAN GRANT

NEWSOUTH

UNSW Press acknowledges the Bidjigal people, the Traditional Owners of the unceded territory on which the Randwick and Kensington campuses of UNSW are situated, and recognises the continuing connection to Country and culture. We pay our respects to Bidjigal Elders past and present.

A NewSouth book

Published by
NewSouth Publishing
University of New South Wales Press Ltd
University of New South Wales
Sydney NSW 2052
AUSTRALIA
https://unsw.press/

Our authorised representative in the EU for product safety is
Mare Nostrum Group B.V., Doelen 72, 4831 GR Breda, The Netherlands
(gpsr@mare-nostrum.co.uk).

First published 2026
Reprinted 2026

A catalogue record for this book is available from the National Library of Australia

ISBN: 9781761170751 (paperback)
9781761179457 (ebook)
9781761178726 (ePDF)

Cover design Amy Daoud
Internal design Josephine Pajor-Markus
Printer Everbest Printing

This book is printed on paper using fibre supplied from plantation or sustainably managed forests.

CONTENTS

‘I gotta use words when I talk to you.’

T.S. Eliot

FOREWORD

VERY LITTLE, ALMOST NOTHING

SCOTT STEPHENS

> 'to fit the maximum of love into the minimum of being ...'
>
> – Vladimir Jankélévitch, *The Paradox of Morality*

As strange as it might seem, Stan Grant found his voice when he decided to walk away from the media. On 22 May 2023, he faced the camera as host of the ABC's *Q+A* program for the last time. He looked worn down. There were signs of spiritual exhaustion in his dim, slightly moist eyes. The years of racist contempt, of filthy slurs and unrelenting online hatred, had done their damage. He made no attempt to conceal the wound. 'Sometimes', he said, 'our souls are hurting.' Speaking to those who had directed their abuse at him and his family, he said, 'if your aim was to hurt me, well, you've succeeded'. His words were simple, and achingly human. But for many, they must have struck a discordant note. This is not what they would have expected. Not from him. Not in times like these. Where was the pride, the refusal to give your enemies the satisfaction of seeing you bleed? Where was the stoic determination to leave the stage undefeated, head unbowed? Sure, he may be bloodied, but where was the fist raised in defiance? Where, at least, was the prophetic jeremiad, the parting denunciation of Australia's original sin, the congenital stain on the nation's soul? Any one of these would have been legible to the algorithms that govern our social-media-saturated lives. They would have appealed directly to the passions that fuel our politics. It was a viral moment waiting to happen.

Instead, Stan did something incomprehensible. Without a trace of bitterness or self-pity, though with evident emotion in his voice, he said he was sorry to have 'given you so much cause to hate me'. And as he went on to explain why his time in front of the camera had drawn to a close, it became clear that he meant it:

> We in the media must ask if we are truly honouring a world worth living in. Too often, we are the poison in the bloodstream of our

> society. I fear the media does not have the love or the language to speak to the gentle spirits of our land. I'm not walking away for a while because of racism … I'm not walking away because of social media hatred. I need a break from the media. I feel like I'm part of the problem. And I need to ask myself how, or if, we can do it better.

In the end, his words seemed hardly to matter. For no sooner had he signed off than the media machine roared to life, turning his *cri de cœur* into yet another *cause célèbre*. The decision to bare his soul became just more grist for the opinion mill. By the following morning, front pages and social media feeds were filled with denunciations of institutional racism in media organisations and displays of solidarity with Stan himself (#istandwithstan, #werejectracism). But however well-intentioned, these various attempts to transpose his tender words into the online vernacular of outrage betrayed their meaning – and ignored his invitation to draw near and sit alongside, in silence and in ashes.

It wasn't long before the chatter surrounding Stan's departure had run its course. And attention did what attention does: it moved on to the next thing. In the silence that followed, his language changed. It deepened and softened. It was at peace. *Murriyang: Song of Time* is his first harvest from the seeds sown during this period of withdrawal. In this miraculous book, he managed to shrug off 'the derisory language of media and politics' and express himself in what Albert Camus would call 'the language of humanity'.[1] Which is to say, the language of love. With *Murriyang*, Stan joined that rare company of writers and composers for whom words and music are not so much opposed to silence as they are the conditions in which it can be heard. Camus is one of them; 'silence, not French', writes Alice Kaplan, was his 'mother tongue'.[2] We could also think of Debussy's *Pelléas et Mélisande*, an opera that uses sound to 'demarcate a space' such that 'silence becomes audible'.[3] The same can be said of the *Nocturnes* of Chopin and Fauré, or of Mompou's *Música Callada*. There is the Norwegian novelist Jon Fosse, whose meditative fiction is a vast, sprawling attempt to 'put silent speech into words' – for, as he said in his Nobel Lecture, it is 'only in the silence that we can hear the voice of God'.[4] And then there is Simone Weil. In one of her letters to Father Joseph-Marie Perrin, she referred to 'a silence which is not an absence of sound but which is the object of a positive sensation, more positive than that of sound'.[5] She would characterise this silence as 'the presence of an absence', a transcendent reality to which the soul is turned in the 'unmixed attentiveness' of prayer.

How fitting, then, that Stan would continue his exploration of the space between words and silence in a book which originated as a series of lectures named after Simone Weil, presented at the Australian Catholic University. On each page, he pitches his voice just above a whisper and 'just below the volume of the news'. There is no argument being prosecuted here. There is no rallying cry. What there is, instead, is the gentlest of invitations – the same invitation he extended on that evening in May 2023: to draw near, to sit alongside, to inhabit the silence, to listen, to learn to speak a different language. I recall a remark made by the philosopher Stanley Cavell towards the end of his life: 'I am becoming freer than ever from the desire to persuade.'[6] *When Words Fail Us* is the book of a man similarly free.

One of Stan's singular achievements in the lectures gathered in this book is to show how the opposite of silence is not music but exhibitionism; it is not speech but self-assertion. Egotism is, after all, inimical to silence. It demands to be heard, even if it has nothing to say. For the French philosopher

Vladimir Jankélévitch, this tendency of the 'I' to be the centre of its own universe poses a precarious moral problem: how to safeguard enough 'self' that one retains the capacity for self-giving love, but not so much that what Iris Murdoch calls 'the fat, relentless ego' overwhelms the moral reality of someone else? On one side, there lies an 'annihilating humility'; on the other, a 'swelling boastfulness'. Avoiding both temptations, Jankélévitch proposes that we embrace instead the disposition of the 'almost nothing' (*presque-rien*) – a form of modesty or self-restraint that tries to remain unobtrusive, that attempts not to be noticed, that directs moral attention beyond itself – which he will variously characterise as a willingness to 'look for the half-light, paint in half-tones, half-say, with a lowered voice'; as being like 'an iridescent soap bubble that quivers and glows for a few seconds in the sunlight'; as resembling a 'fine beam of light'; as an 'internal forgetting of self and an infinite openness to others, vast just as the sky is'.[7]

This will doubtless seem like the kind of moral saintliness which very few could attain – admirable, perhaps, but unachievable. And yet, as the Danish philosopher Søren Kierkegaard insisted almost two centuries ago, admiration is most often a form of moral laziness in so far as it fails to acknowledge that what we admire is meant to make a claim upon our conduct.[8] Besides, the point of saintliness is not to invite detached admiration, as if it were some portrait hanging behind plexiglass in a gallery. The 'almost nothing' of the saint, rather, is like a window: it should enable us to see others in a gracious light, as persons worthy of love. Even those Simone Weil would call 'the afflicted' (*les malheureux*). As Stan puts it, 'To live as a saint is to see the saint in others.' Though I would be inclined to modify this sentiment ever so slightly: to see a saint is to be shown the inexhaustible preciousness of others.[9] For it could be that the saint more closely resembles Walt Whitman's depiction of the poet in *Leaves of Grass*, as the one who sees and shows 'how [people] join':

> He says indifferently and alike, *How are*
> *you friend?* to the President at his levee,
> And he says *Good day my brother*, to
> Cudge that hoes in the sugarfield;
> And both understand him and know that
> his speech is right.[10]

In this scene, notice that the poet does not do anything remarkable, nor are his words especially profound. He doesn't mount an argument for the equal dignity of all human beings or try to persuade others of the evils of slavery. But by addressing president and slave alike with a familiar equanimity, he manages to illuminate 'something so transcendent, so incapable of gradations' in each person that it places them 'on a common level, utterly regardless of the distinctions of intellect, virtue, station, or any height or lowliness whatever'.[11] The poet's achievement is thus to become transparent, unmemorable, as we continue to see the two men in his tender light.

Three years ago, Stan Grant found his voice when he walked away from the media. The abuse he has suffered and the evil he has seen could have made it hard, unyielding, bitter. One could hardly have blamed him if it had. Instead, he speaks like someone who is at peace because he has made his home in the silence. But, of course, he doesn't need to speak and he is not seeking to persuade. He is not clamouring to be heard. That's why his voice has now dropped to a whisper. Very little. Almost nothing. 'Please, do you mind? Will you allow me?' To hear it, you are going to need to come close. Where the fire is warm, and the light gently flickers.

Scott Stephens is the ABC's Religion & Ethics online editor and the co-host, with Waleed Aly, of The Minefield on ABC Radio National.

INTRODUCTION

HE TALKS IN MATHS (WHEN WORDS FAIL)

In one of their most memorable songs, 'Karma Police', Radiohead, the English avant-rock band, call for the arrest of a man who talks in maths. In a world of wordless abstraction without analogy or participation, this man is an executioner who wields the brute truth of numbers. You will get it, he warns us. Don't mess with us. Can't you hear the nightly news? You are a disgrace! Racist! Homophobe! Anti-Semite! Open your borders! Immigration is killing us! Fill in the blanks. I am me and you are you and we can never meet. We do not disagree, we hate. The world of the permanent enemy. Who said the Nazis lost the war? This is the world the Nazi jurist Carl Schmitt foresaw. If you don't know him, you should. Look him up. We live in his world.

'Karma Police' is a song about an alienated existence where we have lost ourselves. We no longer communicate. We buzz in a world of technology, rapacious business, greed, progress and exploitation. What is a simple person to do but to put our hope in some cosmic vengeance. When there is no language of justice, there is but karma.

'Karma Police' is a plaintive, even cold, hymn to a brittle world. A world beyond God. A world of efficiency and human redundancy. A world of mathematical language, a girl with a Hitler haircut. No longer even the unadorned evil of Hitler but the mere appearance and performance of evil. But here's the thing: we asked for it. Efficiency or God? We chose efficiency. We got our wish.

Radiohead is the last note of modern music. There is nothing nostalgic left. There is nothing to miss about us. We exist beyond ancestors or ceremony. Our cathedrals are for tourists. Our lives are metronomic and angular. We're disembodied voices. The beautiful unfinished symphony of our clipped tones and our shattered syntax that in all tongues struggles to say 'I love you' or 'help me' we replace with a tuneless mechanical voice soothing us. Fitter and happier, more productive, fond but not in love. No, never in love. There is nothing left to love. Just things to buy.

To listen to the cacophony of Jonny Greenwood's guitars is to hear the crash of falling ramparts.

The universe is collapsing around us. Can we stop the noise? Please I need to rest. Oh, these voices in my head.

All we have left to respond with is a backwards glance. Oh, so that's who we were. I can't remember. Didn't God exist once? Oh, yeah, God is dead, and we have killed him. Who are we to erase the horizon? Now, behold the last human. The human at the end of time. No art, no beauty, no truth. What is happiness? The last human blinks. We have removed all pain. Whatever we wish is a touch away, even friends – and better still, we need never know them. We are subjects, points to be made in an argument.

God won't save us, but an airbag will.

The man in 'Karma Police' speaks a language of maths. Not maths as possibility but maths as certainty. Mathematical fascism. A world not of tragedy but body count and calculation. Mathematics is an unforgiving, precise language. Maths doesn't lie. Maths can never be wrong. We humans might err in our equations, but the numbers don't. Mathematics has no synonym, no allegory, no allusion. Maths has no sentiment, emotion, hate or love. There is nowhere for us to hide in mathematics. It is an honesty beyond us. We need our lies. We cannot survive without our lies. If I think about it, that may be the best thing about us.

The geocentric model was a lie we needed. Ptolemy and Aristotle both knew this. What a gift, that we humans on our floating rock should be the centre of the universe. To think for all that time the moon and stars circled us. But the truth was circling us all along. Our curse is that we will not leave truth alone. Someone must ask the question and spoil it all. So, we wake one day, and Copernicus has ripped us from heaven. We are not the centre of anything. Just us, just we humans at the fate of the cosmos. That's how it must be, of course, but we will never be the same. We will never again agree on anything. So, humans start a quarrel with God over time. *Shut up, God,* and He does. Now we can blame Him for all that we do. How can God allow this? What a cruel God.

When we get too close to the truth, our monsters come out. Think about Einstein. $E=mc^2$, an equation that helped seal our fate. He knew we couldn't handle it. He warned us but we wouldn't listen. Einstein's most famous equation does not lead directly to the nuclear bomb, but it is a tool to unlock nuclear fission. It is another critical step in our rush to destruction. 'I am become death, the destroyer of worlds.' We are entombed in maths. It is a language that we will never speak.

I was listening to an interview with Cormac McCarthy – a rare one, he didn't speak much in public. He lived far from the lights and the noise. He held up a mirror and gave word to our violence and cruelty. McCarthy preferred the language of science. The great man of American letters had no real use for words. He probably thought we had exhausted them. Anyway, the interview. McCarthy wanted to talk about physics mostly. Then he said something that landed like a punch in the gut, even if I should have known the punch was coming. No poetry, he said. Not anymore. Maths annihilated poetry. We incinerated poetry in Hiroshima and Nagasaki.

He was right. I knew it the moment he said it. He wasn't the first. The German–Jewish philosopher Theodor Adorno said the same after the Shoah. To write poetry after Auschwitz was barbaric, he said. We had no words left. Language was an obscenity. But even then, he left the door ajar. Of course, we could write poetry, but it must not speak technology. Shame is, that's all we did speak. There were exceptions like Paul Celan or Anna Akhmatova and Czesław Miłosz, but I have always felt they were a rearguard defence. Out front were all the ugly people hiding behind a façade of truth or beauty. Bending their words into machinery. Horrible they are. Every time I pick up a modern book of poetry I am braced for inevitable disappointment. Detergent words, literary critic George Steiner called them – that's all they have.

So, McCarthy sealed it for me. No more poetry. Why don't they just say it? Shut up and calculate! Love? Then say love. Don't count the ways. We like to find hiding places in our words. What a discovery was poetry, a language of imprecision. The poet is a liar. Aristotle was 'right': the poet is not an historian who reports what happened. The poet bends words to tell us what may have happened or may not. Plato was even more precise: the poet imitates speech. Poets use words like spells. They enchant us. Keep them out of the city, Plato cries.

If there is no God, if a flower is a synonym, then to hell with truth. Poets are loose everywhere now, serving in parliament, selling dishwashing liquid, clogging up newspaper opinion pages. Don't trust those who use words for affect. Don't trust those who waste words on campaigns. They defile words. Poetry is propaganda; it has been since Homer. Here's what German philosopher Martin Heidegger had to say, and it is worth heeding: 'Actions not words count in the calculus of planetary calculations.' Oh, yes, mathematics people. Measure. 'What use are poets,' he said. With that he may have finished it. Closed the book. But Heidegger could not relinquish us to a world of flat truth. In hope he wrote, 'And yet ...'

There it is, there we are in the 'and yet ...' Don't give up on us, he is saying. Yes, this same Heidegger, a Nazi like Schmitt, holding out something of the human. What a species we are, unattributable to our worst. We are irreconcilable and confounding. Thank God or we would be doomed. We would be merely a number. And yet ... More in the ellipsis than the words. Like Michelangelo's Sistine Chapel painting of the outstretched hands of Adam and God, reaching but not touching, leaving something for us. Here we choose and we have chosen horribly. We could have believed but we wanted certainty. Well, certainty we have in all its destructive potential. But here is an open space. God can't fill it; if He does what's the point? He gave us existence, we do the rest. But there is the space to lie, to live. Where the lie becomes the truth. The only thing that is true, the truth not seen but unseen.

And then ... and then, oh, sometimes, there appears a saint who speaks words she does not earn a living from. Words cannot fill our stomach. We must not take them to market. Do not, do not, fill up on words. They don't come at a price. Words are more precious than gold. In the beginning was the Word and the Word was with God, and the Word was

God. The first verse of the first chapter of the Gospel of John. Why give that up for a number? The word cannot be seen or counted. But it can be experienced. It can be inhabited.

And then ... and then, oh, sometimes, there appears a saint. French philosopher, activist and mystic Simone Weil said she felt Christ enter her body. She did not seek Him. She was racked with headaches, and she sought out pain. She introduced her pain to the pain of the world. She chose to stand with the afflicted. Affliction, that's her word. No numbers in that. No measurement. Affliction is empty. Meaningless. A cold hand of fate. It chills those it touches to their very souls. The afflicted is a thing. No longer human. But here most real, most present to God. Here in affliction, stripped of all personality, most human. This is where Simone Weil found truth, and she died for it.

Weil has affected me more than any other thinker. Take a look at a photograph of her. She appears tiny, bird-like. She was given the nickname the 'Red Virgin' or the 'Martian' because she was considered so cold. So odd. But she was fierce and formidable. She wrote without fear and with a piercing intellect and an unwavering sense of what was right. Above all, she called us to strip ourselves of what she called our 'personality', the veil we put between ourselves and God. Weil's epiphany for me was affliction – affliction that put no value, no meaning in suffering. In affliction we were stripped bare, reduced from a human to a mere thing. And this might be the most honest thing about us. This is when we are present to God.

Weil was thirty-four when she died in a sanatorium in England. She was born to a Jewish family in France, and she fled the Nazi occupation of her homeland. She suffered from tuberculosis, but it is said she died as much from her refusal to eat any more food than was rationed to the members of the French Resistance. It is also said that she was never baptised, although she pledged her life to living in the shadow of the cross. The crucifixion is the truth of the world. She saw in the scandalous death of Christ no meaning, no triumph. He died a thief's death. Jesus knew what this world was capable of, and it was not the measure of existence.

Poet T.S. Eliot called Simone Weil a saint and Weil herself called us to be saints. We misunderstand what a saint is: it is not to be beyond the world but in it. In it all. Not holy, but human. French existentialist writer Albert Camus would have called the saint a rebel. Camus was in thrall to Weil, too. He called her 'the only great spirit of our time'. Her influence is apparent throughout Camus' work. His rebel is the one who says 'no' to the world, but affirms it at the same time. The rebel, seeing the death of God, wishes to renew faith in the world. Here's what he wrote: 'When the throne of God is overthrown, the rebel realises that it is now his own responsibility to create the justice, order and unity that he sought in vain in his own condition, and in this way justify the fall of God.'

Camus was an atheist, or so we conclude. I don't believe it. It is not what his words say. He sounds closer to Christ than many I hear profess to be Christian today. He sees the utter absurdity of what we have created on earth – but didn't Christ also? Is it not absurd that He be crucified for speaking love and forgiveness? Are you a king? asks Pilate. You say that I am a king, Christ replied. But I am not of this world, I am of the truth. And so was Camus. His truth was that we are each other. The rebel is against the 'incompleteness of life'. We do not suffer independently; we are bound to suffering as a collective experience. You could say that our tears are our common language.

Simone Weil and Albert Camus seem extreme figures but only because we are so mundane. We so easily fall into line and pick our side. We are so easily convinced. We are proud of ourselves too. We are so sure of who we are and our morality. It is because we have been hoodwinked into believing that man is the author of man. How ridiculous, but that's what this modern experiment in the human is all about. I think, therefore I am – what madness. But here we are and there are so few like Weil and Camus left among us. There are so few saints. They are still here but we likely don't hear from them. They are content watering flowers and taking walks. One might smile at you when you are rushing somewhere important.

How on earth would we deal with Weil today? She'd be certifiable. We couldn't handle her. We only have provocateurs. That's easy. The dumber we are, the smarter we can sound. But Weil was untameable. She was ferocious. She was courageous. She resisted, no refused, categories. That's another thing we would not like today. We love categories. When I say 'we', I do not mean all of us – likely most of us don't live such straitened lives. But outside in the noise, there's someone waiting to label us. And that's all we will be.

I can't stand it.

Simone Weil said what the human requires is silence and warmth and what we are given is an 'icy pandemonium'. Say that again: icy pandemonium.

She wrote that eighty years ago when the world was at war. It applies today. Different, maybe even worse. We have learned nothing. I reckon we are more brittle today, shriller, colder. Try this: mention God in polite company and watch people twitch. Hell is not hot, that's a myth. Dante took us into the depths of evil and it was frozen down there.

Anyway, why am I writing this? Bit late this far in to ask that. But why? Because damn it, words must matter. Better that they are insufficient. I don't want the charlatans who imitate speech; I want words that mean something. I want words that, when we hear them, let us know it is a human speaking. It matters not one bit that I might not understand the language. This clumsy communication, this reaching for the soul, is all we've got against a cacophonous world. Otherwise, I could talk in maths, but look where that has got us.

Simone Weil believed in words, Camus wrote. It cannot be futile. I hope not anyway. But it might be too late. That I cannot deny. I think that's what Cormac McCarthy was telling us. The curse of the modern age is incomprehensibility. We are a babbling mess. It isn't that language divides us, it is that we speak into a void. We are unhinged. I wonder what it was like before we killed God. We certainly slaughtered one another – that seems baked in. We slaughtered each other for God. But each generation's slaughter is different and now it is so technical, so inhuman, so distant and so complete.

There is so much I could say about how we cannot say anything today. I keep hearing that song, over and over: lock up this mathematical man. The Irish-born philosopher and great admirer of Simone Weil, Iris Murdoch, invited us to consider the existence of a tribe whose private thoughts consisted entirely of mathematical calculations. My God, how precise and impersonal that would be. 'For such a people', Murdoch wrote, 'thinking would be the private manipulation of exposable symbols.' What is she saying? Words are measurement, abstractions of logic, addition and subtraction. All human inarticulacies lost, all yearning and seeking and failing, all surprise, all enchantment or embarrassment gone.

We are not made for mathematical language. 'Language and thought are not co-extensive', Murdoch wrote. Words do not appear from thought like projections onto a screen. Words are the human expression of the mechanical mind. Here's Murdoch's punchline: 'We cannot consider language a set of grooves into which we slip.' Words matter when they come from the soul. Imprecision is our gift. That's why we listen. Listening is the source of empathy, which is the foundation of forgiveness. We do not have to understand each other to understand each other. Well, that's how it should be.

We do not find a human in our words today; we find a subject. Let me try this: What does love mean? In our nation where the most popular television program is a reality show offering marriage at first sight, what is love? Love becomes an amusement park. In everyday speech we filter love through politics, gender and sexuality – even through race. Love is possession and emphasis; love is not what Saint Paul called *kénōsis*, an act of self-emptying. If we cannot speak of love as a simple word of immense meaning, what hope do we have?

This is what happens when we weigh and measure our words. If humans are algorithmic, mathematics has won. Maths speak for us. We are cancelled for the words we use. Some words are awful, brutal, harmful – yet to lose them at the cost of losing beauty is a bad deal. But what am I saying? We have closed that door. Censor them! Burn the books! Silence the speech! The machines will write the poetry. We have entered the realm of the unholy.

Forgive me, I have fled this horror. I am writing this from my haven, a piece of the earth where I hear birdsong, I see mountains and I sit under a tree beside a stream. I can retreat into a library of real books. At any moment I can be in conversation with Jane Austen, James Joyce, Fyodor Dostoyevsky, Niels Bohr, Saint Silouan, Friedrich Nietzsche, Toni Morrison, Patrick White. I can read about physics, philosophy, theology, art. I play records, real records with grooves on vinyl that I must listen to and turn over at the end of each side. Here I can drink tea brewed from loose leaves presented in a teapot. And I take walks in the cooler evening air.

Returning from one of those walks, my wife pointed to a magpie. He comes here every day at this time, she says. He's beautiful. He has no fear of us. I think how untroubled he is by his existence. He calls to other magpies, and they are not confused. It is hard to be a human, I say to my wife. It is the hardest thing we can do now. The human cannot be her own master. The human cannot be so precise. We went astray when we made a God of our thoughts. I am not sure of a lot of things – in fact, I run from certainty. But I am certain of one thing: if we are the limit of the world, we are the limit of the human.

In Euripides' play *Alcestis*, Herakles asks the spoiled prince Admetus: Do you know what it is to be human? I don't think you do. We all gotta die, he said. When you're mortal, you gotta think mortal thoughts. These lectures you are invited to read are my little mortal thoughts. I delivered these in a lecture series dedicated to Simone Weil. Am I a saint? I hope so. We should all be. To be saintly is to be human. Saints are not above the world, saints are as broken as the world. The saint is not perfect – thank you, God, not perfect. My words will be imprecise and real. I hope I don't make sense sometimes. I hope you disagree at others. But when I say 'love', when I say 'tree', when I say 'human', believe me. I mean it. I don't want to live in boxes. Put politics back where it belongs. Politics does housework, Camus once said. That's all. It does not matter to me and you. A smile does, though. Have a cup of tea, a real one, and sit awhile. This is just an invitation.

If this fails, then we are done for. Words fail; murder follows.

LOST IN ENGLAND

This year I have gone wandering through the memories of C.S. Lewis. With a dear friend, I walked the halls of Magdalen College in Oxford. I traced my hands over the walls that Lewis had touched. I followed his footsteps down the tree-lined Addison's Walk, of which Lewis wrote:

> I heard in Addison's Walk a bird sing clear:
> This year the summer will come true. This
> year. This year.

It was on Addison's Walk locked in conversation with J.R.R. Tolkien that, in a gust of wind, Lewis felt the breath of God. My friend and I walked Oxford's cobbled lanes. On this crisp evening in the dying hours of winter, I heard in the distance the tolling of a church bell. In The Grove, I came upon a parcel of young deer, as had Lewis when he pondered Psalm 42:

> As the deer pants for streams of water, so my soul pants for you, my God.

I have come here because I am soul sore. Weary. I seek refuge in Lewis's Oxford, yearning for repose and a place to draw closer to God.

I am in search of words ... words to still the noise. I came to find what Lewis had seen there. Lewis, Tolkien and T.S. Eliot.

There is magic in this place. A magic I so crave that I might find a new way of speaking to a world of tired words.

Here I might lose myself. And find me again.

*

On a drive from Oxford to Cheltenham, about an hour's duration, suddenly, the road was blocked. There were no signs, no alternative routes, and I found myself winding down one of those quintessential English back-country lanes, heavily wooded, incredibly narrow and lined with stone walls. A road on which it is simply impossible to see what's coming around the other side.

I was growing more frustrated, getting further from my destination, not knowing which way I was going. The satellite navigation system kept returning me to where I had come, so I turned it off. After a while, I found myself undergoing a blissful change. I appeared from the forest and into an old village. Really, it was of another place and time. I swore that if I closed my eyes, I could hear people driving a horse and cart. In fact, a woman astride an enormous horse was riding down the middle of the road.

She did not care that there was a car on the road. I saw another couple, lost in conversation over a fence, and I thought, I have landed in an utterly enchanted land, a place that time has not yet entirely devoured. It put me in mind of a beautiful book that I came upon quite by accident in an old bookstore. Its title was *The Crooked Scythe*, by George Ewart Evans, a writer and a former teacher, and he did something quite miraculous. In post–World War Two England, Evans recorded the voices of a people doomed, a people caught in the wash of time. Their way of life was vanishing.

Evans spoke to the blacksmiths, the shepherds, the farm labourers, and the domestic servants. He recorded their simple stories not out of a sense of nostalgia, but simply to show these people were here. They existed. They had a voice, and soon they would not.

Lost in this village down a country lane in a land far from my home, I thought, this is what I need. I need places like this. I need places where I can hold the world at bay. And as Evans did, linger among those who speak more slowly, more softly.

This is why I have come to the other side of the world. I am out of words at home. I have grown bored with my language, bored with my voice, bored with my writing. My words labour under the weight of Australia's history. The land itself, as much as I love it, bears down hard.

Now in another place, I am finding lighter words. At times, I may not need to speak at all. I smile; I nod. I seek permission to speak. Please, do you mind? Will you allow me?

That's the critical part, I think. To seek permission. We do not do that enough in public discourse, do we? We presume our place. We expect our voices to be heard. We demand that we be seen. I have a voice! I must speak! You must listen! So much noise. So many people are talking. Whether we have anything of use to say, we are compelled to speak. The world demands it of us. We must have an opinion.

We hear it all the time. Silence is complicity. There are times when that is undoubtedly true, but these are not those times. Today we talk altogether too much. We are too loud. Silence is not complicity. Noise is complicity. Yes, the noise that looks to divide us, the noise that drowns our compassion, the noise that says, I have a moral righteousness that you lack.

I shelter in silence. Silence is the proper response to the affliction of our age; the silence that emulates Christ on the cross. The silence that does not rail against the world but sighs a sigh of love and forgiveness. Sometimes I think we have lost the meaning of silence. Silence is not non-speech. Silence is its own language.

In words that seek permission, words that do not compete with the noise, we have a greater chance of being heard. And when I say seek permission, I mean to allow our language, our writing, to invite the reader, the listener, in. To pitch our words just below the volume of the news.

To not yell, to not adopt a position, but say with humility: here I am. My palms are open. My heart's open. May I speak to you? May we talk together? Of course, sometimes we must make a stand. We must for the love of humanity say no! But must we do so in haste?

We might find a language that has manners, dignity and decency, and in the gentility of that language, we might make space for each other. Let's invite people to share that space with us and ask permission from them to allow us to speak, rather than demand that they must hear. It is one of the curses of our age that so much writing, so much speech, is brittle. It is flinty. It shouts, it is declamatory, it exclaims, it judges.

And that's not where I wish to be, and that is why I'm here, in a magical place of beautiful words, a tear in time. I am here seeking a softer language in a softer landscape, down cobbled streets and country lanes, wandering, spending time browsing through a bookstore, allowing time to not be set by the clock, to live in what French philosopher Henri Bergson called the *durée* – the time between time.

Let's not rush. Let us sit. Would you mind if I said something?

*

A lifetime of news reporting has led me through the maelstrom. I have reported wars. I have walked through the bombed-out rubble and heard the cries. I've seen the suffering and now I seek a place of withdrawal that is not retreat.

Let us be clear about withdrawal and silence. I do not mean cowardice. I do not advocate apathy. There are those among us who turn their faces from suffering. They do not see the beggar in the street; they step over her to buy their morning coffee.

There are those who, when asked to give to charity, say they give at home. When they hear the cry of pain from next door, they turn up the volume of their television because the tears of strangers are merely water.

No. That silence is the roar of contempt. That silence is betrayal.

But there is another silence of the bowed head. It is the silence of reverence. It is a silence that accepts that sometimes at the sight of the wound, words fail.

Silence is a commitment that the suffering will not go unheard. Silence can say more by standing quietly with the afflicted than by advocating for them. Many a lawyer or activist content themselves with having done their best and move on. But who the next day holds the prisoner's hand despite what he has done? Who visits the victim's family when the mourners have long gone?

Sometimes, in the silence, all we can do is breathe good into the world again.

By withdrawal, I do not say turn off the news. Sadly, it is unavoidable. The withdrawal I look for is a smile, a bird in a tree, a country lane, that horse ambling down the road.

Here I may find something to say that is an antidote to the noise of division and conflict, hatred, judgement, and everybody yelling. And for me, at least, to try to find a place, not of retreat, but one where people may find me rather than me chasing them.

That is just what George Ewart Evans did. He was a teacher and a writer who fought in the war and returned to civilian life a little broken and depressed. He found his repose in the smallness of village life in East Anglia. As the world sped up, he slowed down. He paid attention. He was available for beauty. He listened. And people spoke to him. In *The Crooked Scythe*, he does something quite miraculous – he quietens me. In his book, I am not alone.

I meet people of the most delicate resistance. Priscilla Savage – or Prissy – a kitchen girl on a big farm. She went away 'foreign', as they say, to work in a doctor's house in Essex. She returned and married a farm worker and had her children and they lived on twelve shillings a week and Prissy baked bread in a brick oven.

She told Evans how she heated the bricks, cleaned out the ash and put the dough a-settin-in. Nothing happened during a-settin-in even the doctor tending the kids would have to wait outside if the oven door was closed.

No bread had the flavour of home-baked bread, she said.

And Sam Friend of Framsden, a farm worker all his life except when he fought in World War One. He was a homespun philosopher, Sam. In his day some of the young'uns didn't have to eat. Food is like digging a hole and putting in some manure. 'You're bound to get some growth, ain't you? Well, I say the young'uns today have breakfast afore they set off and a hot dinner when they come home.'

'These young'uns,' he said, 'kinda got the frame. That is it. If you live tidily that'll make the marrow and the marrow, make the bone' – or 'the boon' as he called it – 'and the boon make the frame.'

Ah, the language. Simple. No fuss. Words that put on no airs for anyone. Words that require no translation. Words that make plain sense.

The people in Evans' books live. It is as though they know they cannot compete with history, so they lower their voices, they smile not too often, just enough, and to the world's toils they shrug.

For these people, time moves by the sun and not the clock. Lives are seasonal. Pleasures are quaint. Evans tells of the houses of local folk, all the same, two bedrooms, a small kitchen, a dining table, a cosy living room. A battered comfortable chair. Reliable clothes.

Possessions are practical rather than fashionable.

Evans describes how one could swap houses with another and still feel at home. But there was one touching detail: each house had a small thing of beauty, a china cup, a porcelain doll, or an animal figurine.

There must be beauty in life. How much better if that beauty is modest.

I read George Ewart Evans knowing this time has already passed. Technology made people redundant. Changing workplace laws tilted the balance of relations between employer and employee – yes, mostly for the better – but still even in positive change we lost something old and good; something decent.

Evans was no sentimentalist. 'Any attempt to "fix" a village in the past', he wrote, 'to preserve the old ways and customs artificially, is misguided romanticism, wrong in its conception, and impossible in its application.'

The village, he said, 'has never stood still'.

He's right you know. Do not trust nostalgia. It is the refuge of scoundrels and tyrants who do not respect our memories. In our wistfulness they see opportunity. There is no greatness to reclaim. The people of *The Crooked Scythe* knew that. They did not live in the best of times; they just lived in their time.

Still, when I read their stories, melancholy overtakes me. Evans is walking through the afternoon of things. So am I. That's what draws me here. I don't want the past back, but maybe I can just stay awhile, here in this fading light.

V.S. Naipaul dwelled here too for a while. He was an orphan of an empire like me, and like me lived among empire's ruins. In the stripped bare trees of English winter, Naipaul saw intimations of his mortality.

The Trinidadian Indian-British writer journeyed into village England to search for truth and beauty beyond the vicissitudes of history or race. In his autobiographical novel *The Enigma of Arrival*, Naipaul looked for enchantment in postwar England's decay. 'How tenuous, really,' he wrote, 'the hold of all these people had been on the land they worked and lived in.'

Naipaul saw people shaping up to the world. He wrote of how his character Jack died asserting the very act of living.

George Ewart Evans did not pine for the glories of old England. Certainly, he had no time for the monied class. His politics were a lot more to the left. But in yesteryear, he saw lessons for us today.

We should resist the seduction of time, not let

the noise lure us. We should meet people where they are, in their soft places where time does its work on them, we should let them talk as they do and there we should sit and listen. Because ... just because.

*

George Ewart Evans did not champion triumph. He was not interested in the heroic deed. He just chronicled the little voices of a crumbling world. This was a poetry of darned socks and a battered pot on an open fire. It was the last testament of a passing people. Beyond here is sophistry. Words that have no meaning. Beware of the charlatans. Plato warned us about those who enchant with their clever words. They flatter our ego, our delusion. These are the politicians and poets who look to bring order to the world.

We should not trust them.

These charlatans lurk in the lowest parts of the soul; a shadow world, the *eikasia*. Here, the images on the cave wall are a mere illusion. This is a world of appearances. It is a world of flash and show. In rhythm, metre and harmony, Plato said, these poets see things only through words, rather than the eye of the soul.

Mighty is their spell.

'We can admit no poetry into our city, save only hymns to the gods and the praises of good men', he wrote.

Beware of Homer, who called us to worship the immoral gods and whose language bewitched us. 'If you grant admission to the honeyed Muse in lyric or epic, pleasure and pain will be the lord of your city ...'

For Plato, there has been, from old, 'a quarrel between philosophy and poetry'.

For Plato, the philosopher holds out the possibility of purification of the soul, of a return to the transcendent good.

In philosophy, Plato says, 'We practise dying', and so we learn how to live. The philosopher king keeps the possibility of a transcendent justice. The poet is a false know-all, he says, who can merely imitate talk. The artist is a gossip.

Art conspires with pleasure to deliver us not justice, nor wisdom but mere semblance. The artist is the enemy of virtue. Yet the fallen human is more prey to sophistry than truth. The truly philosophical life returns us to the good we knew before birth, beyond earthly existence.

For Plato, God is the only true artist. The cosmos is his art. The separation of humans from the cosmos is the end of myth, the end of truth. It is the beginning of human time, and time steals our words.

This is a punishing vision to be sure. Iris Murdoch, who appropriated Plato's ideal of the transcendent good, the unity of perfection, the source of all truth that lies beyond the struggles of the human, wrote that 'it may be said that Plato is a puritan and this is a puritanical aesthetic'. There is in Plato, Murdoch said, 'an almost vehement rejection of the joys of the world'.

Murdoch said Plato had plenty of reasons for thinking poorly of humankind. Yet she absolves him of resentment. Plato reached for a higher order – to Plato, 'God, not man, is the measure of all things.'

When we have strayed so far from the divine, is there even poetry today? Have we buried poetry in the cold storage of our brutal history?

Theodor Adorno told us that to write poetry after Auschwitz was barbaric. 'Even the most extreme consciousness of doom', he wrote, 'threatens to degenerate into idle chatter.'

After the Korean War and Vietnam, the bombing of Cambodia, after the Balkans wars, Rwanda, the 9/11 attacks on the United States, the civil war in

Sudan, conflict in Yemen, the first and second Congo wars, Ukraine, Hamas' attack on Israel on 7 October 2023, after the devastation of Gaza. On and on and on. After the untold millions of dead, disfigured and displaced, where is poetry?

Is it all just idle chatter? Is poetry buried in newsprint and television commentary? What literary critic George Steiner called 'detergent emptiness ... uniformity and jargon'.

Where is poetry when the poets speak the propaganda of politicians? When poets are activists. When poets scrawl their words on placards at a protest. Where is poetry when everyone with an attitude is a poet? When poets populate the opinion pages? These poets are like the sophists of Ancient Greece; they use words for effect.

I hear everywhere the poets who imitate talk, telling us what to think. Poets of moral outrage. Poets who pick sides. Poets who choose their humanity. This is an age of anger, we are told. I think more likely that we have fallen under the spell of angry poets. They have loosed a contagion, and their anger infects us.

We are angry because we are bereft of simple words. There is a poetry after Auschwitz, and it is the poetry of tears. It is the poetry of prayer. It is the poetry of a candle lit for hope. It is the poetry unwritten and unread.

Simone Weil said that a cry cannot express itself in coherent words, 'the words that try to translate it fall completely short'. Pondering Plato, Iris Murdoch said, 'Written words are the helpless victims of men's ill will.'

'Writing can easily become a kind of lying', she said.

George Ewart Evans did not favour drama or embellishment in the lives he recorded. He simply let them speak, these poets who bake bread, who work fields, who raise children and, in a world that may overwhelm us, quietly, dutifully affirm life.

That is the true poetic response to a world of disappointment, to do more than we say.

Where is that poetry today? There is too much identity. Too much politics. Propaganda. Poetry is sophistry. Words that need to convince. Are poets charlatans? I think so; far too many, at least.

Am I one of Plato's purists? Then yes, I am one of Plato's purists. Poetry cannot be the plaything of our vanity, our politics. Poetry cannot be written for persuasion. There is a place for the true poet, but it exists beyond the chatter of daily life.

We must bend to hear true poetry. We must lean

in. True poetry whispers. The poet does not raise her voice. The true poet knows that truth is in the smallness of things. Poets who do not need flash words to tell us what is right and what is wrong.

Poets like Oodgeroo Noonuccal, who echoed Plato when she told us that we are born to know the good. In our hearts we know that hate is wrong. Poets like Russian Anna Akhmatova, a poet of self-effacing beauty. Poland's Czesław Miłosz, who told us that poems should be written rarely and reluctantly, under unbearable duress and only with hope.

Or like former US poet laureate Tracy K. Smith, who blocked her ears to the noise:

> I don't want to hear their voices.
> To stand sucking my teeth while they rant.
> For once, I don't want to know what they
> call truth.

The poet responds to the horrors of our world not by drowning them in the semblance of words, but by putting something of beauty back in. I have in mind the poet of silent music, Estonian composer Arvo Pärt. He never gives interviews. His voice never rises above a whisper. But in his music – what he calls the tintinnabuli, the little bells – he evokes a sense of the divine that lifts us above the morass of the hatred of the age.

Pärt's is a music of immense smallness.

So, we choose. This is what we must do. Like Arvo Pärt, I choose to turn down the volume. This is my response. There are enough people making noise, but Pärt's music holds open a space for us where the noise is quelled and all that is left is a muffled sob.

Are we putting in something of beauty as a response to the world that will nourish us? Or are we seeking only to match the noise and the volume of hatred with our own noise that spreads the contagion of anger, which is vastly different to righteous anger?

Words amuse us today, those words that cannot bake bread or till a field. Words that do not fill us up because the words themselves are already too full. But life is not words. We do not speak life, we live it. Critical theory is no substitute for calloused hands.

Tracy K. Smith knows we are too small for history. Were we not so small history would be unbearable. In her poem 'The Nobodies', she writes:

> They rise from the dawn and dress.
>
> They raise the bundles to their heads
> And their shadows broaden –

Dark ghosts grounded to nothing.

They grin and grip their skirts.

They finger the gold and purple beads
Circling their necks, lift them
Absently to their teeth. They speak.

A language of kicked stones.

And it's not the future their eyes see,
But history. It stretches
Like a dry road uphill before them.

They climb it.

These are my people, the nobodies. These were George Ewart Evans' people. I have stepped out of my world into a mythical England so that I might hear again the words of the nobodies. So I might find words worthy of my father who worked his life in sawmills and who with my mother walked the dry hill of history.

*

So, what am I doing here walking in the footsteps of C.S. Lewis, lost in a country village, wandering among the ruins? I am here because I am haunted. Haunted by a memory of an England that entranced me as a boy. An England I had never seen.

I breathed in England from afar, when I heard the wistful strains of the Kinks' song 'Waterloo Sunset', about a boy at a window looking out onto the world below where he needs no friends because he can gaze on the Waterloo sunset and then he is in paradise.

I am here because I am haunted by the memory of a man from long ago – a man who saw the strangers of another land come to his home, who saw a world fall, who lost his words and had to find a new way to speak when all of his truth was a lie. He had thought that the ocean's horizon was the limit of the world, but he saw a ship bring strangers to his country.

In a few years, he boarded a ship himself and went to England. He saw the new world born. He entered time. I am in England to write a novel of his story. I cannot write it in Australia because Australia will trap him as it traps me.

I am chasing a myth, but one I need. I cannot think at home. I am still reeling from the sheer volume of the Indigenous Voice referendum. The brute noise soured my words. I began to recognise in myself a snarling face of truth. Just being an Aboriginal person lost its enchantment. It lost its meaning.

I do not want to count myself among the sophists and charlatans who believe that words serve power.

I am here to attend to the world, not to shout at it.

I am here so that my wounded words might heal. I am here to be silent.

*

Simone Weil wrote that 'every time there arises in the depths of a human heart the child-like lament that Christ himself could restrain, "Why am I being hurt?", there is clearly injustice'.

Our response to that cry should not be revenge, law or rights. It should not be politics or recognition. The response of the human is love. This is the response of the divine within us. It is the response of silence.

Modernity has set the limits of horror. We are harried and prodded. Weil said that what we need is a warm silence, but what we receive is an 'icy pandemonium'. No, silence is not always complicity; right now silence is the only way we may hear the cry of the afflicted.

Simone Weil, like Plato, recognised that it was time that severed us from God.

In Ancient Greece, Plato saw the death of myth. The poets no longer spoke to the experience of life. They were charlatans who used myth as a semblance of enchantment.

They 'steal away our souls with their embellished words', he wrote. In time without God, we are slaves to history. We have no word for God. We have nothing meaningful to say. Today we speak into a technological void. We are disembodied voices in cyberspace. Friends without faces.

Time strips us of our souls. We replace the soul with a mirror.

Weil shivered at this tyranny of time. 'God is not in time', she wrote. 'We are alone in time.'

In the world of human time, what we celebrate as liberation, the freedom from all hierarchical truth, even from the once supposedly cast-iron laws of physics, is really an invitation into a world of confusion. We have created a world of babbling incoherence. A world of choice beyond truth.

We have unlocked heaven only to enter our own hell. Weil writes: 'Today it is as if we have returned to the time of Protagoras and the Sophists, the time when the art of persuasion, of which slogans, advertising, propaganda through public meetings, newspapers, cinema, and radio constitute the modern equivalent, took the place of thought, ruled the fate of cities, and caused coups d'état.'

But, she warns, 'it is not Greece, but the terrestrial globe, which is at stake. And we want for a Socrates, Plato, Eudoxus, the Pythagorean tradition and the teaching of the mysteries'.

There is of course the Christian tradition, she says, but it can do nothing if we do not come alive to it once more.

We have surrendered the spiritual to time. We have made ourselves subservient to time. In time we have become immune to our suffering. Weil warns that 'we cannot one day recover what we are missing unless we feed within our whole soul the extent to which we have deserved our fate'.

We have blindly entered servitude. As Weil writes: 'If someone offers himself as a slave on the market, is it any surprise he finds a master.'

*

When I look at a picture of George Ewart Evans, I see a man who personifies his language. There is a gentility and a dignity to his bearing. He carried himself against time, just as he watched time absorb an entire way of life.

The poets today look to put the world in order. Evans looked to honour it. The poets today seek to save the afflicted. Evans looked to attend to them.

Time. Time is the great revolutionary force. Time as efficiency, time as productivity, time as machinery, swallowed the lives of the people of *The Crooked Scythe*. When you have lost your world, you have nothing left to say.

You are a memory. You only ever will have been.

That is the beauty of George Ewart Evans. He gave these people a final word before their voices were forever silenced. There will come a time when we have nothing left to say and silence is our epitaph.

TO ASK THE HOLIEST QUESTION

In one of the tellings of the Grail myth of twelfth-century Arthurian literature, the wounded Fisher King is beyond hope or help as his body wastes so does his land. What can heal him and restore the kingdom?

Only the goodness of a knight, without ego or desire, one who may ask the holy question: what are you going through?

The Grail is a myth that takes us to the heart of compassion. The knight does not inquire, what is wrong with you? What can I do for you? Who did this to you? Is there justice for your wound? But simply, what are you going through?

It is a question that invites both the king and the knight to surrender something of themselves. The knight seeks no gain from the question, and the king must answer without pride.

Indeed, the king surrenders his crown to the humble knight.

Similarly, for the faithful only this question leads us to God. This should be the most human question. Why? Because this is what Christ bled for. For all my life I have felt the presence of Christ. Being a person of faith is not belief for me, it is real. As a boy, I was raised among the Aboriginal churches of New South Wales. We were the people of the frontier missions. Christ was not a colonising God; He was as real as an ancestor. More than that, He was the living creator God.

There was no separation between my culture and my faith. We are a mystical people, and mine is a mystical faith. Each week at mass, I enter a place beyond human reason. In the Eucharist I partake in the blood and flesh of Christ. Not a symbol, but the living presence. As I have grown so has my faith. It has been tested in history. It is my faith to which I have turned when confronted with the horrors of the world. As a journalist, on the front lines of war and disaster, I have seen evil. Evil has a face. So does love, and that is where I see God.

On the cross, Christ suffers for us. In his pain, He asks us, *What are you going through?*

If Simone Weil teaches me just one thing it is

this: when I no longer ask this holy question, when I can no longer hear the other, I am no longer human. She means to truly hear. Not selectively. Not hear the cries only of those we call our own, those we choose to recognise, but to hear even the cry of those I might call my enemy.

This is the gift of sainthood that Weil places before me. The saint who is not beyond the human but the very fulfillment of what is human. The saint who refuses the unreality of the world. The saint who attends to the soul of the other. The saint who cries too.

To live as a saint is to see the saint in others. Because our cry of pain, of abandonment, is the cry common to us all. It is our only truly shared language. Even laughter is suspicious, cruel or mocking. But a tear is all we have left when we have nothing left to say.

This cry I do not hear with my ears, I hear it from the silence where God dwells. Where the Word – as John tells us – was with God and the Word was God. None of this is easy; were it so then we would not need to talk of God at all.

I cannot speak of Simone Weil without speaking of God. She would have it no other way. She would rather that God is all I speak about. As she writes, 'Only God is of concern, nothing else is.'

Yet I cannot help but notice how it has become fashionable, even preferable, more palatable, to speak or write of Simone Weil without mentioning God at all. Instead, we get Weil the thinker, the rebel, the woman, sometimes the so-called self-hating Jew, perhaps Weil the mystic, but not Christian. Christ is an embarrassment. It is as if some simply do not know what to do with all Weil's God 'stuff'. It is too weird.

But Simone Weil's weirdness is her gift. When she says, 'Christ himself came down, and He took me', I believe her. Not metaphorically, not symbolically, not imaginatively, but physically. Christ entered her body.

The words she speaks come directly from Christ. I feel He did not just enter her body but also spoke through her. She is communing with the crucified Christ at the foot of the cross. There she sits with the entirety of the universe. Once Christ has possessed her, she is no longer of this world. Truth, she knows is not in our minds, or our words. Reason and speech have become an assault on God.

God waits.

God is far and near, as far and near as our souls. The distance between ourselves and our souls is the distance between heaven and earth. There is a screen placed between us and God, Weil says. God gives something of himself up to create room for us. He withdraws so that we can be.

Without God, Weil is just another thinker – interesting enough, certainly provocative, sometimes poetic but often flippant, ill-thought-through, impulsive, maddening and contradictory. She is not especially original; much of her thought she owes to Ancient Greece, especially Plato. But it is God who sets her apart. She goes where Plato cannot. There are moments when Christ speaks through her. She is the voice of heaven.

Weil came to Christ through her pain. Throughout her life, Weil was plagued by blinding headaches. Although agnostic she retreated to the Benedictine monastery of Solesmes where she sat through services for eight hours a day. Each word, she said, struck her like a blow on a raw nerve. She wrote that she came to understand 'the possibility of love despite pain and suffering'.

But it was not until later that she felt the physical presence of Christ. He merged with her spirit while she was reading a poem, English poet George Herbert's 'Love (III)':

> Love said, you shall be he.
> I the unkind, ungrateful? Ah my dear

I cannot look on thee.
Love took my hand, and smiling did reply,
Who made the eyes but I?

Love is the order of the world. Not the love of our desire, our ego, our personality. Weil says we must love necessity – that means everything we love will die, will rot. Necessity, she writes, 'makes all our love objectless'. Necessity is our one and only enemy, and for that reason, we must love it. Without that, there is no love.

And we must love that which exists beyond what we could even imagine existence to be; we must love God. God, she wrote in her notebooks, 'has inscribed his signature in necessity'.

All that I love, I know can hurt me. Love today will be the pain tomorrow when that love is gone. Lost to the world. Or lost in the world. And yet we love, we must. For me, that means loving as we love God who may be so far because we cannot find our way home to where He is: right here waiting inside us.

Love, Weil writes, 'is a divine thing. If it enters a human heart, it breaks it.'

Weil's God is hard to find. Hard to love. He is an absent God. He has abandoned me to my time. We are alone in time. We decided that God could have eternity, we would be lords of time and time has become our battleground. God has left me to do my will as He must. 'Necessity', Weil writes, 'is God's veil.'

He loves me, so He leaves me.

'The absence of God is the most marvellous testimony of perfect love,' she says.

Weil tells us, if God is in my life, I will not seek Him. God's presence will obliterate my desire for His presence. What good to be a mere shadow in God's puppet play where I am not free to fail? What God does not give me the freedom to hurt?

When I cry out for God, when I am in the desert, when I weep, when I wail from that part of myself where words fail, then I hear Him.

Then I am at the foot of the cross. The ultimate silence of suffering. Where Christ says, 'It is finished.' This pain of living and the cruelty we inflict, it is finished. Life is not finished but life without God is finished.

At the cross, God returns me to the Good, to the One, to the truth beyond our truth – to the eternal forms, as Plato tells me. To the moments before my first breath when I already knew what evil was and what good was. Then I know, there in all the suffering that the world can do to me, in its insult, in its wounds, in its vinegar bitterness, I know that that is not the measure of me. It is not the measure of us. That may be the measure of the world, but God is greater than what we humans can do.

Even if humans can kill God.

There at the cross, I know that there are no words for hate. There is nothing to impede forgiveness because there is nothing to forgive. That's what I have misunderstood about forgiveness. I have thought of forgiveness as a negotiation, a give and a take. Forgiveness I have twinned with atonement; I cannot freely give it without expecting something in return.

Forgiveness I have seen as the most divine gift – something supernatural, beyond me. However much I might wish otherwise.

It is hardly surprising then that forgiveness is so difficult. Am I alone in this? I do not think so. We know not what we do. But we miss that the true gift is that we are released from it all. We are cleansed in His sacrifice. Our debt is paid. That's why there is nothing left to forgive.

Christ has taken it all on himself, the utter meaningless cruelty of the world.

Meaningless? Yes, Weil says.

This is the truth of *malheur*: affliction. Affliction is a word that Weil takes and sears into our minds.

Never again will the mere word 'suffering' suffice. Affliction is degradation, humiliation, tinny coldness and, most chilling of all, indifference. We cannot bring ourselves to hate or pity the afflicted – the one who is not worthy of human emotion; not human at all, merely a thing.

Affliction is indiscriminate and random. Natural disaster, revolution, war visit torment, and death on the just and unjust, on the poor and the rich. As a news reporter, I have seen it. More cruelly, as an Aboriginal person, I have experienced it. In an instant, the lives of an entire people and their descendants down the ages were up-ended, because we were simply there.

The afflicted are anonymous. The glorious idiosyncrasy of human life is erased. The afflicted have no names. They are always 'them': oh those poor Afghans, the Jews, the Palestinians ... 'our' Aboriginal people.

I am a figment of your imagination. You know me before we have even met. My history has already spoken for me. And you will speak for me, or against me. Even you who wish me well would have already decided who I am. I am speaking, yet who is hearing? What are you hearing? Am I expected to confirm what you already know about me?

What do you need from me? That I be the Aboriginal person you imagine? Or the person I am? I am me. But to you, I am one of the afflicted, the nameless, whom you reserve the right to name.

I will not re-enact history. I do not want to die again and again. I do not want to die for your imagination. I do not want to die for your sympathy. I want to live so that I do not need your sympathy.

I do not want to die for those of my people, fellow Aboriginal people, who will obsess on death. They want back what the world cannot give them: time. They have fallen prey to the great conceit of modernity: the death of God. There is no God they recognise left to pray to, so they pray to history.

Such people are trapped in modernity's jail; justice cannot break time's chains, justice can only beg time to be released.

History is the God Hegel made. A vengeful, slaughtering God whose cruelty is the price we pay for our deliverance. History is time's wager: it will all be worth it in the end, no matter the body count.

Time shook Aboriginal people from a divine slumber.

For tens of thousands of years, a people lived in this land without the desire for history. No writing, no memory, no trace of the modern shibboleth of becoming. There existed a being, a unity with the One; we painted that on rocks and told it in stories not written down because they were living stories, not history. Our stories did not place humans at the centre of the universe. That was before modernity started a quarrel with God over time.

Now, like all people of modernity, we are a people of desire. Desire for recognition, for truth, for justice. Plato saw the same in Ancient Greece and warned that all humanity is left with is semblance. The myth is gone, and the new myth is pedalled by charlatans and sophists. Poets who only imitate talk. They speak to convince.

I do not wish the enchantment of their words.

But here is the curse of the afflicted: there are no words. Weil says affliction is inarticulate. It is we, speaking for the afflicted, those we imagine – we want to make sense of it all. Someone must pay. We think revenge or rights or recompense might be something approaching a fair trade for suffering. But affliction, Weil writes, is a word beyond human thought.

To acknowledge affliction is to confront that it may happen to us for no reason and no one may pay. We must accept, she says, that what we are 'might be abolished and replaced by anything whatsoever of the filthiest and most contemptible sort'.

The afflicted are the breathing dead. Affliction, says Weil, 'freezes all those it touches right to the depths of their souls ... They will never believe again that they are anyone.'

Weil's description of affliction shocks me into the truth of my complicity – all our complicity. In any major city, on any day, human misery is simply factored in. Confronting the face of suffering we cross the street or turn our heads or reach into our pockets for the least we can afford.

In my comfort, in my reassuring affluence, in a New York café, I absent-mindedly drop a glove to have a stranger pick it up and with a smile return it to me. Yet on the same day, I sit in a train carriage of people who avert their eyes from a woman with no toes, frostbitten and bedraggled. A woman we would call a beggar because our words for what is human are exhausted. We look away and I look away too.

Weil's shocking truth is that the beggar could so easily be us. The beggar could so easily be God.

God waits for us, she says, 'like a beggar for our love. The stars, the mountains, the sea and all the things that speak to us of time convey his supplication to us. God is only the good that is why he is waiting there in silence.'

We are out of words for God as we have no words

for the beggar. At best we throw the beggar – God – our loose change. And then we rail against injustice, we march with outrage for the suffering people of the world that we never have to see. We never have to touch. We might not like them if we get too close. People are too human up close. Better they are an idea, an avatar, an abstraction. Better that they are something to march for not sit with.

Simone Weil calls me to account for my conscience. If she offends me. If I leap to defend my conscience, my morality, then Weil would ask me where that conscience, that concern for suffering, is, when I so easily step over the afflicted before me. How convenient it is to simply not see God. How righteous it is to insert politics, or moral vanity, for true love.

Like Dostoyevsky's woman of little faith in his novel *The Brothers Karamazov*, I can love the world yet love no person in it.

The beggar is too close. She breathes on us. And we cannot bear it. Better that people suffer at a distance. Then their suffering is grand. Their suffering has meaning. And the awful truth is that those who suffer – the afflicted stripped of personality – bring meaning to our lives. There is no meaning in theirs.

So, it is for Christ on the cross. We turn Him

into an idol and the cross into a symbol. It is not enough that He dies wordless. He must triumph. This is a denial of the truth, that when Christ died, He died in infamy and barely noticed. His followers were hunted and afraid. Anything but triumphant.

Those far from the cross will write of Christ's triumph. Just as today suffering grows grander at a distance.

For Weil, the crucifixion is ridiculous. In his affliction, Christ died the death of a common criminal, a death sentence of thieves. 'It was not til Christ had known the physical agony of crucifixion, the shame and blows of mockery, that He uttered His immortal cry, a question that shall remain unanswered through all times on this earth, "My God, why hast thou forsaken me."'

This sends a jolt through me. Weil shocks me by how she strips the crucifixion of its glory. People of faith have so wanted to invest this moment with a triumph worthy of God. Christians often rush to Easter Sunday; they want the resurrection and not the three days Jesus spent in hell. Weil, heretically, tells us she has no need of the resurrection. The truth of Christ is on the cross.

Weil's description puts the tortured face of Jesus, like the beggar, before our gaze in a way that dares us to look away. Here is a man of sorrows, his body wracked in pain, his lips parched with thirst, his face smeared with blood and his head adorned with thorns.

Weil takes us closer to a Jesus who feels what we feel. This is the Jesus of doubt, even doubt of God, and a Jesus of fear who in the darkness alone pleaded 'Father, take this cup from me'.

Jesus is not the all-powerful, all-seeing God, but God beneath our contempt, undeserving of our pity. A God so small we could kill. Christ died, Weil wrote, because he was 'only God'.

Only God.

And the Aboriginal person is only an Aboriginal person. The Afghan is only the Afghan. The Jew and the Palestinian are only the Jew or the Palestinian.

The beggar is only the beggar.

Yet in her affliction, the beggar is closer to God. There is no vanity, no ego, no desire to separate her from the truth. Not that her suffering makes her more worthy; it makes her nothing at all. We are something – too full of something. We cannot even look at her.

The beggar should pity us. Simone Weil writes:

> There is a class of people in this world who have fallen into the lowest degree of humiliation, far below beggary, and who are deprived not only of all social consideration but also, in everybody's opinion, of the specific human dignity, reason itself – and these are the only people who, in fact, are able to tell the truth. All the others lie.

The Christ on the cross is stripped bare and rendered nothing. He is not the saviour that He will become. He is yet to adorn walls and cathedrals. In that moment, the world turns its eyes from Him. His suffering has no meaning. We are wrong to exalt His suffering, that is to make an idol of Him. Then He is beyond us, something of worship, rather than someone to know. To love.

In that moment of death, Christ is small. He is so small that He can appear in a tear. Only in that smallness, that we might not look away. Then we might hear. Then we might hear the cry of others.

They will not be figments of our imagination. We will not look for in their misery our magnificence.

We might ask then, the question of the Grail: what are you going through?

*

Johann Sebastian Bach opens us to the wordless scream of an abandoned and tortured Christ. The German philosopher Hans Blumenberg, writing about Bach's *St Matthew Passion*, said, 'The Passion is not a martyrdom, hence not a piece of evidence for a truth. Bach is not a "missionary". He does not let Jesus die for a cause.'

Bach knows, like Simone Weil, that Christ does not need evidence. Christ was not dying for a truth that needed answers. When Pilate demanded of Him, 'What is truth?', Christ fell silent because He knew that to speak would give too much meaning to that question.

The truth was standing in front of Pilate, yet all he had was a question. So begins the modern quest to make truth unrecognisable. Modernity cannot bear silence, so we answer Pilate's question for him. The truth is not God's truth; the truth is whatever we say it is.

If it is evidence that we look for then surely, we would abandon the world, because the evidence by now is overwhelming that we have no love for the world. We have piled up so many bodies and when confronted with that awful truth, we respond with the language of rights, recognition, democracy, history.

What Weil called words of the middle region because the words of a higher order – God, love, justice – are too dangerous for us to say.

If evidence swayed Bach, he would not have written a note. He would have concluded that we were not worthy of beauty.

Bach was born into a world shadowed by catastrophe, forty years after the Peace of Westphalia ended the Thirty Years War. The Wars of Religion devastated Europe. Armies pillaged and burned villages to the ground. Entire populations vanished. Bach's biographer, John Eliot Gardiner, says the land shaped the composer – the dense Thuringian forests. This was a haunted landscape. Gardiner describes it as an abyss. Spooky: 'the emptiness of the primeval forests', he writes, 'with its undertones of demonic power unleashed by the long war'.

Death shrouded Bach from his birth in a war-torn land and the early deaths of his children. Only ten of Bach's twenty children survived into adulthood. Gardiner says that so many of Bach's later works explored this dichotomy 'between a world of tribulation and the hope of redemption'.

Bach composed because in his music that horror would not be all that we are. The Christ that Bach gives us is St Matthew's Christ of so few words.

A Christ who is silent while everyone else taunts. A Christ who cries his abandonment, then a final wordless cry, then dies.

Blumenberg says, 'One can see how the text of Matthew, so congenial to Bach, almost fades into nothingness. Bach's music is the very sound of Christ's silence. He makes it so quiet, that now we might finally hear.'

Blumenberg says Bach turns 'listeners into witnesses'. He reactivates the ability to listen.

Music exceeds poetry because it transcends the limitations of speech. At its best, when it hews to silence, music needs no translation.

The French philosopher Vladimir Jankélévitch knew this. 'Where speech ends, music begins', he said. Jankélévitch was the greatest writer about music of the twentieth century. Like Plato, he was mindful of the charlatans, of the artist who seeks to bewitch us with his dazzling ability.

Jankélévitch was wary of perfection. 'It lacks nothing', he wrote, 'and yet it lacks something.' Everything is present but the heart. Simply, he said, this music 'lacks soul'.

Music calls us to do – to listen, to play, to live. Music calls us into time itself. The written word freezes time. Once it's published, we can pull a book from our shelves and return to that moment of creation. Yes, it can enliven our imaginations and may at times set us free. The listener rewrites the music. In performance, the player transforms it.

Jankélévitch asks, where in the end is music? Is it in the piano? Is it in the vibrating string? Is it in the grooves of a record? That may be its source, but we hear it in the air. Once music is played it is released.

'Music', he wrote, 'is not calligraphy projected into space, but a lived experience analogous to life.'

Music is a dance with time. We live music in time. We experience music in time and music can return us to time – not as it was but as we remember. Music once heard is gone, but its perfume stays, the scent of all memories: joy and heartache and regret. We cannot merely write about music as we cannot merely read about love. Just as we cannot merely name God.

For Jankélévitch, music devoid of artifice, flattery, or persuasion is a music of charm. Charm he calls lovesickness, the 'transfiguration of an inspired heart'. When we hear with our heart, music is beyond words; at the borders of silence it says what is unsayable.

Silence is not the absence of sound, it is not non-speech. Silence is what Vladimir Jankélévitch called a 'second hearing'. In our silence we hear the distant voice, which does not come from a far-off land but, Jankélévitch says, comes from 'inside us'.

It is the 'inaudible voice of absence'.

Silence is the true response to the cry of the afflicted: why are you hurting me?

Silence is the language of the saint. Simone Weil told us that the world requires a 'mystical activism'. It is an activism of attention. For Weil, to attend is to wait upon.

We wait upon the afflicted, as God waits upon us. How different is this from an activism that is greedy, noisy, full of imagination and virtue? Mystical activism asks not how can I fight for you, but simply – and this is so much harder – what are you going through?

Arvo Pärt embodies Weil's saint. He gives daily thanks that as an artist he fails. Pärt's response to the world is to thank God for his failure. He builds a monastery of his music and invites us to pray too. Describing his music, Pärt says it is akin to 'spiritual fasting', an escape into 'voluntary poverty'.

Spare and meditative, Pärt's tintinnabuli evokes a chant, with a repetitive arpeggiated triad echoing the sound of a bell. Pärt says it emerges from his 'dark hours' when he searches for answers to a 'complex and many-faceted world' that confuses him.

Everything outside of this one thing, Pärt says, 'feels as if it has no meaning'.

Listen to Arvo Pärt's 'Fratres (Brothers)' and hear how the composer contemplates the space where everything unimportant falls away. 'Time and timelessness are connected', Pärt says. 'The instant and eternity are struggling within us.'

In the Garden of Eden, time begins in an act of human defiance. In the fall, humans enter our time. So, I believe, God must wait for us beyond time.

Perhaps Vladimir Jankélévitch would describe Pärt's music as an echo of God. God, who 'does not come with the noise of wrathfulness but as imperceptibly as a breeze'.

Pärt's is a music of interior voices, an invisible harmony. It is a music of silence that Jankélévitch says allows us 'to hear another voice, a voice speaking another language, a voice that comes from elsewhere'.

This 'unknown tongue ... hides behind silence just as silence itself lurks behind the superficial noise of daily existence'.

This is 'the most secret of all musics'. Music that, for Jankélévitch, pacifies 'the monsters' in us all. But do marauding armies not march to a beat? Did Goebbels not swell satanic Nazi bloodlust to the soundtrack of Beethoven, Wagner and Bruckner?

How could a Germany that could give birth to Schumann also give us the Shoah. Jankélévitch would never forgive them. Never again would he speak or write about the genius of Mozart or Handel or Brahms or Strauss. Not, he said, because he was a Jew but because he was a human being.

It sounds so noble, yet something in it disturbs me. Jankélévitch, who wrote so beautifully about music, more beautifully than anyone I have read, denies himself some of the most beautiful music ever composed. I can't help thinking that Jankélévitch betrays music and he betrays humanity. Why should the Nazis own Bach? If we cancel evil, evil doesn't die. We do. We deprive ourselves of beauty, our defence against the evil in us all.

There is something too grandiose about Jankélévitch's *ressentiment*. Something that foreshadows our censorious, morally vain age. He stops listening to the God he writes about. He refuses redemption. Rather than the soul-affirming possibilities of music, Jankélévitch locates his morality in the shrivelled soul of history.

If we deprive even monsters of God's love, if we deny even monsters Bach, then Christ died for nothing. Bach didn't write only for those saved, but for the possibility that we might all be saved.

By denying himself German music, Jankélévitch finds himself uncomfortably but unavoidably on the side of everything he despises. The world is poorer. The monsters win.

He shrinks the world to the size of hate. How very modern.

Today our morality is a morality of refusal, of denial. Our conscience is too conspicuous. It is a triumph of a philosophy of critique that, in its desire to excise evil from the world, strips it too of the good, the true and the beautiful.

This is a philosophy of Nietzsche's last man, who would sooner have a world of mediocrity safe from offence than let loose our passions, lest it risk annihilation. There is no future there. We will still have Goebbels among us, for tyrants thrive in the grinding monotony of a life without beauty. Yes, we will have Goebbels but no Beethoven or Bach to let in God.

To quote Jankélévitch back to him, who will pacify the monsters in us then?

To deny the world anything in it is to refuse to love the necessity of it all. Simone Weil says, then in that necessity we can be free of it and closer to God who is necessity. The best music says yes to the world, all of it, and calls me to say yes too.

And here among modernity's 'icy pandemonium', in the most unlikely places, we might hear the voices of saints.

So it was that I found myself with a hundred thousand people in London's Wembley Stadium, all singing with one voice to the rock band Oasis. This is admittedly a more profane artistic experience than the music of Bach or Arvo Pärt, but it was no less sacred.

There is something ineffable in the musical charm of the band's founding force, the brothers Liam and Noel Gallagher. Together, the deceptively introspective lyrics and the irrepressible melodies of songwriter, Noel, and the outsized but accessible charisma of lead singer Liam, are magical.

The brothers are famous for their public feuds. The acrimonious break-up of the band disqualified the possibility of reunion. When they walked out, arms around each other, to the deafening roar of the crowd, all cynicism vanished. This was not, as some sneered, all about the money. This was about life.

The band's music is an affirmation of the possibilities of existence. Their song titles – 'Live Forever', 'Wonderwall', 'Rock'n'Roll Star', 'Don't Look Back in Anger' – speak simply to the joy of being alive.

In their charm, Oasis turns us away from the mirror to look into the eyes of each other. Here, together, we find our souls, our chosen land. Oasis conjures their Kitezh, the mystical Russian city submerged so that the Mongols could not torch it.

It is immortalised in the opera composed by Nikolai Rimsky-Korsakov. According to myth, under the water we can still hear music. Kitezh, an invisible city, preserved from our hate, still there if we can but listen.

Inside Wembley Stadium I am in an invisible country, a mythical land of dreams, a place beyond the map.

Oasis brings an idea of Britain alive for me, an unlikely Aboriginal Anglophile. It has been my family's fate to dwell in the dark shadow of the British Empire. That is Australia's burden. Here, though, history slackens its hold.

I realise I am homesick for a home I never knew. I am nostalgic for a time of words with no cunning or guile. Words with lilt and vernacular. The Gallaghers still speak with a little wink of their native Manchester. Words that put an arm around me.

Our words are smarter now, more self-aware, yet for all that slippery somehow. We lay words like landmines that blow up on us.

Let us be clear, though. Mancunian patois, like all local languages, masks secrets. Words draw a curtain over the crimes inside the house. The Gallaghers know that – they endured family violence. Their father was abusive or absent.

But here is where they are greater than Jankélévitch the critic. They take that monstrous voice of their raging father and sing it to a hundred thousand people, who will return with their voices: now I hear you. What are you going through?

There was a moment when Noel Gallagher sang a song of regret, of words spoken that we might wish we'd never said, of life little by little draining away. As the song swells to the chorus, I can hear his father – so human and broken himself – when his son sings the line of regret, that he didn't mean what he said, he steps back from the microphone and the audience, as one, finishes the chorus for him.

It is okay, we are saying. We have hurt too. All of us here have lived with pain. All of us have tried to hide. But not now, we hear you. We are all released. We are all forgiven, the greatest forgiveness of all when there is nothing left to forgive.

The artist honours the audience by disappearing. He is not singing to us; we are the song.

In a crowded Wembley Stadium, I know that Albert Camus is wrong: the long human dialogue is not at an end. Here words make another stand.

In a stadium of strangers, none of us is alone. In a world confused by too much translation here the heart listens. Amid this glorious crowd, I find a silence, deep inside, where I can hear my heartbeat.

This is how we answer history. By shrinking. We are too small for history. When we rise to meet it, we stir the monsters inside us. We are the nobodies poet Tracy K. Smith whispered about. The nobodies who rise each day with their lives strapped on their backs, for whom history unfolds like a dusty hill and they climb.

How we need poets like Smith. She is the poet Plato would have cherished, who reclaims simple words from the charlatans and sophists who use words to flatter and enchant. They only imitate speech.

Smith's prayer for America is that amid the metallic metropolis, the grinding noise of 24-hour news, the disappointment of opportunity, the drugged-up drudgery of pain-filled life, there might still be a place quiet enough and small enough to live in.

Smith's is a voice older than America. Too old for a new country of reinvented humans, and language with no past. A country that has slaughtered itself for impossibility. I can understand their words, but I don't know what they're saying. A country where

Seinfeld's Manhattan cruelty exposes our own. A show so cynical, witty, and entirely about nothing cannot but make us laugh.

It is not America we should blame, but ourselves. America is our creation. Our Enlightenment dreams of a rootless utopia. A metaphysical tussle with God that Nietzsche finishes with his declaration, 'God is dead and we have killed him'.

This America is Plato's godless, wordless republic that Austrian poet Rainer Maria Rilke warned us of a hundred years ago:

> To our grandparents, a 'house', a 'well', a
> familiar steeple, even their own clothes,
> their cloak *still* meant infinitely more, were
> infinitely more intimate – almost everything
> a vessel in which they found something
> human already there, and added to its
> human store. Now there are intruding, from
> America, empty indifferent things, sham
> things, *dummies of life*.

America's gift is the gift of loneliness. Not to be known but to be unknowable. To vanish into the crowd, swept along by progress. To whom knows where.

America is a land of relentless becoming.

Being and becoming are the twin poles of modern existence – a Scylla and Charybdis – on both sides there is danger: a totalitarian rootedness of being and a totalitarian nothingness of becoming.

Rilke calls us into the abyss between being and becoming to save ourselves. We must risk it all, confront our will that makes the human an object. The world we think protects us, gives up our unshieldedness – Iris Murdoch would have said to 'unself' – and turn to the open. Rilke's open is not the air and sky and space; it is the vast innerness.

Simone Weil would have said this is the daring of the saint.

William Faulkner, among America's letters great gifts, was so right and so wrong when he wrote about the past not being dead. History arrives in America, but America buries it. In America, the past is assuredly dead, they only have a relentless future.

America's future is coming at us at warp speed. Having reinvented the human, soon the human – what we have recognised as human – will be no more. The mastermind of Google, the inventor of tomorrow, Ray Kurzweil, says we have entered the singularity. It stands for, he says:

> The culmination of the merger of our biological thinking and existence with our technology, resulting in a world that is still human but that transcends our biological roots. There will be no distinction, post-Singularity, between human and machine …

It is unstoppable. In the twenty-first century, Kurzweil says, we will not undergo a hundred years of change but 20 000 years of technological progress.

Martin Heidegger saw this future. 'This day is the world's night,' he wrote, 'rearranged into merely technological day. This day is the shortest. It threatens a single endless winter.'

Heidegger warned: 'The world becomes without healing, unholy.'

When we consider that Heidegger himself fell under the sway of the technological brutality of the Nazis, one can only imagine that he finally captured a glimpse of his own dark heart.

Ray Kurzweil says this new world will need a new religion. Kurzweil is asked if there is a God. No, he said. But there will be.

The world becomes the object of the human, and the human becomes the object of the machine. No matter what atheists may claim, humans have always needed a God. From ancient times a yearning for a higher power is in us. Now God, who has withdrawn so that we might be, who died at our hands, watches a new God born.

The human voice, the word falls silent. The machines speak for us now. No music. No poetry. Just the imitation of beauty. Why have you forsaken me? we might ask.

But listen now to the buried city of Kitezh. Listen for Arvo Pärt's little bells. Listen for Bach's lament. Listen for a hundred thousand voices in Wembley Stadium. We are still there.

And in that watery silence, it is where Simone Weil says God pierces our soul. He takes our hand, she says, and squeezes it.

Then we might hear Him ask that holy question: what are you going through?

TRUTH BEYOND TIME

Once there was a great flood, and it destroyed almost every living thing. Only some people survived. Then came the Ice Age and the people who survived the flood turned into stone. Then creation began again. The spirit beings walked back to their homes and they put down a new pattern. They started life again. Something else happened. A spirit called Marrul walked to a place of holy water and dragged himself to a shelter and died. Marrul sacrificed himself for his people. The people ate his flesh; they were baptised in holy water and entered a new life. The people were reborn through the love of the spirit whose sacrifice gave them life.

This story was told by a man known as the Keeper of Creation. Bungal David Mowaljarlai was a Ngarinyin man from Western Australia.

This was his story of the Wandjina, the mystical spirit, creator of land and people. The story of flood and sacrifice, of a God who dies and washes us clean with holy water to give us new life sounds familiar.

Because it is. Mowaljarlai was in touch with a divine truth of the universe.

He saw visions of God, he walked with Jesus in the desert, and he returned he said with a message for not just his people but all people. Mowaljarlai saw the rupture of time when God dies, and we live in darkness until we return to the source of all creation. Until we are reunited with the creation of the universe.

I met Mowaljarlai once when I was very young. He shook my hand, and I felt as if I was pulled into another dimension beyond the laws of the universe. I felt as though he entered my soul. Mowaljarlai had distant eyes and a face that appeared untouched by gravity. He was a man of sight. A mystic. He despaired at time. Mowaljarlai saw that time – historical time – steals our souls.

The mystery of time has up-ended existence. It has banished God – the divine. Time has made us creatures of our own creation. Time is the great flood. It washes away existence, leaving us submerged in the backwash. Tangled among the debris that we call history. Time has spawned history, and we are all in its grip.

I want us to think again about history. Understand that it is not events. It is not the past. History is an illusion. It is a fairytale to keep away the evil spirits of modernity. There are so many lies told about history, like that those who do not remember the past repeat it. No. I have covered too many wars because we remember the past too well. History lives in us, that is another lie. No child is born with history – we add that later. Far too often, I have seen history as a poison in the blood of identity.

Here's another lie: telling the truth about history will heal us, that it will deliver justice. If we think we find justice in history, think again. If we think we find truth in history, think again. At the risk of being called a heretic, I have no need of history at all. History is about power and progress, and David Mowaljarlai warned we should be wary about that.

I want us to think again about the terms that we simply accept *ipso facto*. Terms like reconciliation, rights, identity, sovereignty, recognition. I want to probe what we might really mean – even if we do not realise it – when we talk of truth-telling. What is the provenance of these uniquely modern shibboleths?

This is a new language of politics and rights. It has its place certainly. Politics is crushingly unavoidable. But it does not deliver happiness – far from it. The evidence suggests we have created a world of greater alienation and isolation. The great mystics like David Mowaljarlai have helped me see beyond the horizon.

To peer beyond the veil of time.

*

The American writer David Foster Wallace, at a commencement address at Harvard, told a joke.

Two young fish are swimming, and they pass a larger older, wiser fish. The larger fish says, 'How's the water today, boys?'

They swim on and one youngster turns to the other and asks, 'What the hell is water?'

Time is the water we are swimming in. Like the young fish we are still asking: what the hell is time? Time is the big one. Time leads to questions about creation which lead to questions about a creator which lead ... well, to us really. All of us here.

Think of this. If God created all, did God create time? If so, is God in time? Is time bigger than God? If God is not in time and we are, do we know something God does not know? Are we God?

Now we are in the deep end.

Saint Augustine in his *Confessions* asked, what was God doing before He created time? He was creating hell for the overcurious!

I am obsessed with time. Time bedevils me. It pursues me.

In *Hamlet*, Shakespeare writes: 'The time is out of joint, O cursed spite that ever I was born to set it right!' I was thrust into time that up-ended our dance with eternity, and I am cursed by the minutes and hours that add up to history. Before we can talk about history, we must ask, what is this revolution of time?

In the seventeenth century, Irish Archbishop and mathematician James Ussher laid the genealogy of the Old Testament over four thousand years of creation and deduced that time began on 22 October 4004 B.C. Yes, that precise.

And while we may chuckle today, we are still no closer to solving the riddle of time.

The Austrian–German philosopher, Edmund Husserl, said thinking about time is the most vexing question – we bring meaning to time; our experience shapes time itself. Yet time shapes our experience. Physicists debate the reality or existence of time itself. To some it is the thing that is most real in our universe. We all move through time. To others, time itself is an illusion. Some see the universe as happening all at once, all things past present and future in simultaneity. Others dismiss the idea of the universe existing within a box as such and argue that it is free of all constraints of time and space. The Big Bang was not a singular event but an event within events.

Now with all this we might be wondering whether we are here at all. Believe me, you are. The clock is ticking and as you read this the minutes will pass. But that is not time. Clocks don't measure time, clocks measure clocks. Right now, someone is reading this in Adelaide or Perth or London, but the clocks tell us it is a different time.

Time appears to move forward like an arrow through space. This is because of entropy, the second law of thermodynamics, which tells us matter moves from hot to cold. A hot cup of tea will in time cool. An egg dropped on the floor will break. We age. We get wrinkles. Our bodies break down. Physicists, though not all, accept that at the beginning of the universe there was order that becomes disordered as it grows. This is the illusion or the experience of the passage of time. But does it have to move forward?

There is nothing in physics that says it is impossible for the hot cup of tea to spontaneously heat up. For the shattered egg to reassemble. Time experiments mathematically work in reverse. Physicists call this 'retrocausality'. The future can influence the past.

*

What if I told you that merely observing a particle in one location – say Melbourne – at once changes the nature of another particle in London? Physicists call this entanglement. I simply pluck a harp string here and in London someone dances. Welcome to the weird world of quantum physics. Albert Einstein called it 'spooky science at a distance'.

A couple of years ago I fulfilled a lifelong dream and visited the Niels Bohr Institute in Copenhagen. I tell you what the scientists do there defies the laws of nature. In fact, they are rewriting those laws. Bohr was one of the founding fathers of quantum physics. Bohr gave us one of the riddles of the universe – what he called complementarity. The act of measuring an object changes the way the object behaves. There is no single picture of the universe; we must see it all in its totality to begin to understand.

Yet foolishly we think we can reduce the world to politics or to race or history or identity. How can we see our common humanity when we cannot see beyond the limits of our own existence? Entanglement. Complementarity. What we do to one we do to all.

Einstein thought this was getting perilously

close to the mind of God. In a conversation with Bohr, Einstein protested that God does not play dice, to which Bohr replied, 'Einstein, who are you to tell God what to do?'

*

More Indigenous people must study physics. It is a window into the magic of time and creation that Indigenous people have inhabited in our stories.

Mathematics orders our world. Yet it is a language most of us do not understand and a language that can wreak destruction. It can be beautiful, or it can be cold and amoral. The principles of mathematics have determined lived reality since Galileo heretically proved we are not the centre of the universe. Newton's laws of gravity set the contours of our political lives. Where do you think we get the idea of nations? Of sovereignty? It appears from political and religious upheaval derived from a scientific revolution stretching back to Copernicus.

The seventeenth-century Wars of Religion – the Thirty Years War that laid waste to Europe – led to the Treaties of Westphalia, which set up the modern nation-state. Today we do not appreciate how modern states derive from gravity – the effect of equal and opposite force. Like Newton's pendulum balls, the states would attract and repel each other returning to equilibrium.

Einstein moved beyond Newton's laws of absolute space and time and gave us relativity. We experience time relative to our mass, location and velocity. If we move quickly through space, we will be younger on our return. Did you know that our head is older than our feet? Quantum up-ends it all again. Imagine what sovereignty looks like in a world where time and space collapse? In an entangled world what does a border mean? We think of sovereignty in terms of legal recognition of land, but sovereignty has already left earth.

We already live in cyberspace. We trade, connect and communicate beyond our nations. Think hard about this. Any Indigenous treaties in Australia had better look beyond land. They must be twenty-first-century quantum treaties not tied to seventeenth-century Newtonian political gravity.

*

Why all this talk of stars, gravity, God and mystery? Because I am tired. Exhausted from a world of politics that has torn us from each other.

I so want to re-enter an enchanted space.

The German sociologist Max Weber called modernity a 'disenchanted age'. It is even better in his native German. *Entzauberung* – demagification – we have broken the magic spell that connects us to the transcendent.

We have surrendered our souls to the machinery of modernity. Ours is a life of efficiency, technology, bureaucracy. Ordered and productive. Remarkable too in its own way – penicillin, dentistry, air travel, Netflix. But when do we gaze at the stars? I have needed to look into the heavens.

I have spent a lifetime at the coalface of our history. I have wandered the world as a journalist chronicling the worst we can do to one another. I have seen more human misery than anyone should see and much more than I could cope with. I am still plagued by nightmares and too often sleepless nights.

Two years ago, as our country wrestled with its own soul in the Voice referendum debate, I walked away from journalism. I don't wish to relive it here; I have worked too hard to create some soft spaces to put my soul to rest. But I will say that my family and I underwent a prolonged and vicious campaign of hatred, threats of violence that challenged my hope in the goodness of our souls. I was becoming a person I did not wish to be.

Words failed me. Words were not enough. A career in words left me with nothing to say. For months I retreated into numbers – into mathematics and science. I found there a beauty and a purity beyond the worst of our hate.

There is a view that science is rational and cold. That science has killed God. Yet, to me, science peers into the mind of God.

This is God as medieval theologian Saint Thomas Aquinas told us. It is *ipsum esse* – the act of existence. The Nobel Prize–winning physicist Werner Heisenberg said that the first sip of the cup of science will make you an atheist, but God waits at the bottom of the glass.

Mathematics is a world of dreams. And a world of nightmares. A world where we dwell beyond what holds us down. It is a place of thought and possibility. There is something poetic, artistic, in the elegance of a mathematical equation. The baffling combination of symbols, letters and numbers that can open the door to a hitherto unexplored reality or perhaps something so utterly beyond reality.

In a museum in Oxford there is a blackboard on which Einstein wrote his equation for the theory of general relativity. There it sits on a wall, as beautiful as a Botticelli. A testament to the possibilities and, yes, the dangers of our minds.

When I walked away from journalism and hosting the ABC's *Q+A* program, I took a drive out to where the country of my father and the country of my mother – Wiradjuri and Kamilaroi – meet. I stood in what the American philosopher William James called 'the specious present' – the prototype of all conceived time. All times present. I stood under a blazing canopy of stars. A dance across eternity. The Milky Way wrapped around me so close I could touch it. I felt all the stories of my ancestors from here and from other lands: all in me. And I was not who I was but where I was.

I was where I needed to be.

*

It was during that time I came upon David Mowaljarlai's poem from his mystical book, co-written with Jutta Malnic, *Yorro Yorro: Everything standing up alive*. Mowaljarlai felt the crush of time;

he felt it rob him of his place beyond the universe. All he had was a whisper against the deafening roar of the modern world.

> Once I was past and future,
> Now I am only the present,
> Today, the moment, And that is hard to bear,
> With no past, no future.

In his art, poetry and philosophy, Mowaljarlai inhabited no time at all. 'Once I was past and future' – not I *had* a past and a future. He lived in a quantum space of entanglement and complementarity. He feared for the future of his people; he watched the old stories go – 'old men die', he said, 'and all knowledge will be dead: gone – we'll be left to live with nothing'. Mowaljarlai wrote that he felt crushed by time – a new measurement of time: history.

From the moment I read his words, they have never drifted far from my mind – I am haunted. Mowaljarlai was speaking from an annihilated place beyond the end of days – death is the worst thing that could happen – living is hell. He had seen the end times, and his torture was to go on living:

> Once I walked my country
> But lost my place
> Then I lost my dignity – spirit.

Mowaljarlai saw God leave the world when modern time appeared. Historical time is the thief of eternity. It is the curse of a modern world where we are forever stepping into now. Mowaljarlai lost his place – time swallowed past and future; that is what was so hard for him to bear.

> The old-time people who knew that big story had died many, many years ago – I say we got no hope of ever knowing it now – these anthropologists can only study, but they wouldn't know where everything is written into the Country.

Old-time people.

I hear Mowaljarlai and I hear my father, who told me a story about his grandfather, a law man of the Wiradjuri. Old grandfather Budyaan had been through the Burbang – he had entered the sacred space of deep learning. He carried the marks of wisdom on his body.

He taught my father dance and language but

when Dad asked him to be taught our law, the old man said no. It is finished, he said. I cannot help but feel devastated by that. Not that it was finished for him, but maybe it is finished for us.

That is what Mowaljarlai was saying.

Mowaljarlai knew, my great-grandfather Budyaan knew, felt captured in historical time. Whatever we do now we do in history.

Now I am only the present,
Today, the moment ...

*

There is a place in the universe where time ends. In the stars. There is a region of no return where massive stars collapse into a singularity. A cooling star is unable to support itself against its gravity, and everything inside the collapsing star becomes trapped behind a boundary called an event horizon. Nothing escapes – not even light. Time ends. The brightest stars die screaming in a void; in space there is only silence – the voice of God.

The physicist John Wheeler called these dying stars 'black holes'. Even he struggled to accept what he saw. 'I just didn't like it', he said. Stephen Hawking postulated that the number of black holes may be greater than the number of visible stars – more than a hundred thousand million in our galaxy alone.

But we need not investigate space to find black holes. History is a place where the human dies screaming. We expel all light, and we are sucked into a vortex of despair. Are we not too shrunk into a singularity where our identities are trapped?

Is history not our event horizon?

*

In his book on Aboriginal religion, William Stanner, the outstanding Australian anthropologist, makes a brief but utterly intriguing reference to his time among the Murinbata people in the Northern Territory.

He describes them as a people with no history. To our modern ears that sounds almost shocking.

It shouldn't.

Earthly life, he revealed, was a cycle 'between mystical source and mystical goal, but there was no final cause or final end'. Not that there was no belief in what we might call an afterlife; there was a conception of spirit-beings, but there was, Stanner wrote, 'no move towards an end that would consummate history; indeed, there was no true sense of history at all'.

When Stanner asked about historical events, particularly a clash between Aboriginal people and Europeans, he found that 'important episodes had altogether dropped out of mind'. This was so stunning that Stanner could not really process it. He simply moves on. Stanner really could not grasp Aboriginal notions of beyond time. But of course, to exist beyond history makes sense.

History requires time. Here there was simply no time. There was tradition, there was ceremony, there was repetition. Life was inseparable from the universe, creation. All things all at once. Stanner gets close to that with his description of Aboriginal time as an *everywhen*. Some suggest it is circular. I think both descriptions fail because they still reference time.

In our age, when we invest history with such moral weight and contest, to be without memory, to be removed from history, is scandalous. It is tantamount to non-existence. Everything in modernity is forged in time.

A people without history, we will consider not a people at all.

*

To be without history shakes our ideas of 'collective memory' or 'collective identity', also utterly modern inventions. Until very recently in human history, they did not exist. We take those ideas for granted now.

I wonder if they are helpful at all. When I think about memory and identity, it recalls something Franz Kafka once wrote about a cage in search of a bird.

I step warily into history. To me, it is like holding shattered glass. Truth-telling may be a project invested with virtue and righteousness. Yet truth-telling is a very modern shibboleth. It has taken on the status of the sacred. It is liturgical.

I do not doubt the efficacy of truth. Our stories, for too long buried, need to be told. If we fail to remember we bury our dead twice. But history is not a destination. It has no place in my future.

When we talk about history, we need to know we are not talking about truth. We are talking about progress and politics. We are talking about a radical reinvention of time that has promised utopia but also sealed the tombs of countless populations.

*

Before World War Two, the German-Jewish philosopher Walter Benjamin, walking through a Munich market, came upon a mono-print by the artist Paul Klee. Benjamin bought it and it became for him a talisman.

Benjamin hung the artwork on the wall of every apartment he lived in, including when he fled the Nazis to Paris. Benjamin would eventually take his own life. History pursued him to the end.

The artwork was called *Angelus Novus* – the New Angel. For Benjamin it became a powerful symbol of history. He wrote that the angel's eyes 'are staring, his mouth is open, his wings spread. This is how one pictures the angel of history. His face is turned toward the past ... he sees one single catastrophe which keeps piling wreckage upon wreckage'.

The Angel of History is a harbinger of doom; its eyes forever turned backwards to a time of catastrophe that defines everything that comes after. The Angel of History threatens to trap us in its wings. History steals our souls. The *Angelus Novus* says no to the modern idea of history as progress.

*

History is born out of the scientific revolution of time. Science up-ended folk notions of time or even timelessness. People were unsettled. Reality as they knew it was turned on its head.

The German writer Aleida Assman, in her book *Is Time out of Joint?*, tracks the emergence of a new story of time. She writes: 'As the time of physics was being cleansed of all human values, experiences and cultural values, a concept of historical time ... began to emerge.'

History as we know it is an Enlightenment project, that eighteenth-century explosion of thought that elevated rationality and reason, that sought to marry philosophy with science to put human destiny into human hands. It was a time of revolution in America and France that set the contours of modern democracy. It was also a time when time itself started again. The clock was reset.

The German historian Reinhart Koselleck nominates 1770 – the eve of the French Revolution – as ground zero for this new historical time. It is also the year Captain Cook claims these lands for the crown. Time was in Cook's cargo. This modern historical time was the most revolutionary force of all. It shattered Aboriginal cosmology – our understanding of the universe and our place in it.

*

Today we are thoroughly historical beings.

As Indigenous people, we cannot find ourselves except in reference to some historical event, some linear time, that had no hold on our ancestors. No longer can we say that we are people with no memory. Unlike Stanner's study of the Murinbata, I would say we are cursed by too much memory.

We are living in Mowaljarlai's unbearable times. And that makes us numbingly modern. As much as some may seek to resist the West or modernity it is – for good and bad – the water we swim in. When we look to make ourselves known, when we seek recognition, justice, truth, we are locating ourselves in the modern invention of history. When we speak history, we are speaking in a tongue foreign to our ancestors. It is a language of eighteenth-century European philosophy.

Hegel, the German philosopher of history, set us on a journey of time towards a utopia – an absolute spirit, a unity and zenith of human possibility. To Hegel, history was a 'slaughter bench, upon which the happiness of nations, the wisdom of states, the virtue of individuals was sacrificed'. But Hegel made a wager. He believed that history would wash us clean of our bloodshed. History would redeem us. It is a dangerous idea. Hegelian historicism would be used to justify the gas chamber and the gulag.

The American political philosopher Michael Allen Gillespie says that after two world wars, genocide and nuclear attack, the hopefulness of the so-called new world found vindication in American postwar prosperity and the recovery of Japan and Europe. 'The future,' he said, 'seemed an open road to the social justice of a great society.' The prophet Hegel appeared to be right.

But it is unsustainable dream living in the shadow of potential nuclear destruction and a progress whose open road is littered with human debris. Gillespie concluded, 'Each step toward prosperity is also one step nearer annihilation – our increasing ability to please ourselves has been matched only by our increasing ability to destroy ourselves.'

Gillespie traces the emergence of history as the imposition of human freedom over nature. Science redefined time and history became the measurement of our ability to control time. History, says Gillespie, 'is human actuality'.

Religion is no longer a unifying force. How do we measure morality? The German philosopher Immanuel Kant believed that reason could resolve its own contradictions. Instead, reason becomes entangled in those same contradictions. To Hegel the French Revolution was a triumph of free will. Humans bend nature to human reason. Freedom is not simply an effect; it is its own cause. Freedom is its own God. History is its scripture.

Spirit and nature are reconciled in history. God is dead but God rises from the dead in history. Look at our world and history does not release its grip but tightens it. Humans are redundant. History is a struggle for power.

Gillespie says 'we today have no cosmology or theology to fall back upon that we can give meaning to our lives. God is dead or at least distant in our moment of need, and nature is a mere mechanical causality whose only end is entropy'. Gillespie warns that if history is chaos, we surrender to nihilism.

We must, he said, question the very ground of history itself.

*

'Once I was past and future, now I am only the present.'

I hear the echo of the words of David Mowaljarlai in a book I read about the Apsáalooke 'Crow' Indian Chief Plenty Coups. Before his death, he told his biographer that when the buffalo died, 'the hearts of my people fell to the ground, and they could not lift them up again. After this nothing happened'. Nothing happened: time had stopped. The world turned, the years passed, but nothing happened.

Bungal David Mowaljarlai or Chief Plenty Coups: I know that I share with them this loss of eternity. I know that politics has no answer to this collapse of the spirit. Politics is part of the problem. History holds no answers. Just madness.

Mowaljarlai and Plenty Coups are talking about trauma. Trauma has its own time.

In a bookstore in Rome, my wife saw a copy of *Trauma and the Memory of Politics* by the British political scientist Jenny Edkins. It is one of those books that called to me.

She says traumatic events freeze the flow of time – trauma breaks from what she calls the linear movement of time that we associate with politics. Trauma time, Edkins explains, is a time of betrayal. It is not only that something catastrophic has happened, but also trust is broken – not just in our fellow humans but in the universe itself.

'Time,' Edkins writes, 'no longer moves unproblematically from past through present to future. In a sense, subjects only retrospectively become what they already are. They only ever will have been.'

They only ever will have been – think hard on that. Only ever will have been. That is one of the saddest sentences I have ever read.

There is the echo of Mowaljarlai and Plenty Coups in the words of my great-grandfather Budyaan. We cannot say that those ripped out of time – the victims of history – are sealed in the past, because there is no past just as there is no future. There is just the event happening over and over and over. The poets know this: history, a nightmare from which we are trying to awaken.

*

If modernity is about tomorrow with all its pain and hope, then to be trapped in today with our hearts on the ground, with a weight too hard to bear, is a cruel curse. We become a thing – no longer human at all.

Simone Weil, a mystic like Mowaljarlai and Plenty Coups, spoke of the afflicted, those irredeemably wounded. She said the afflicted suffer the cold hand of fate that chills them to their bones.

Linear time – the political time of the nation-state – moves on, but for the afflicted Crow, buffalo always lie dead on the plain. For the afflicted Mowaljarlai, the creator spirits have left the earth – time immemorial collides with time industrial. There is the rupture. No past, no future.

Mowaljarlai described a severed spiritual connection that left us adrift – all of us, not only Aboriginal people, trapped between past and future, shrouded in darkness, caught in a never-ending today.

The only way to heal ourselves, he saw, was to put aside time and reason and law and return to God – the divine – beyond us, but who speaks to us and lives within us.

'Everything is represented in the ground and in the sky. You can't get away from it because all is one, and we're in it. As you see the Milky Way it ties right across the land, like a belt.'

When Mowaljarlai wrote of his 'dark night' of the soul, I heard the echo of Saint John of the Cross, drawn into a pit of despair to be stripped of his soul so that he might find God. Rowan Williams, the former Anglican Archbishop of Canterbury, said our world resembles the 'pit' we are in, what we might describe as a 'dark night' for intelligence: 'We don't quite know,' he wrote, 'what knowing is for.' We are swimming in water, and we do not know what water is. We are trapped in time and physics has reset reality, if there is such a thing as reality at all.

Our world feels up-ended. We are left to ask, what is truth? History is modernity's answer, but a history that reduces us to a struggle for power and recognition. We have lost the language of the soul. If we look to history for our soul, we will not find it.

When we speak the words of identity, truth, reconciliation, we are speaking the language of history. We are strapped to Hegel's slaughter bench. I am not saying there is no place for the political. I'm not saying identity, truth and reconciliation are not necessary. God knows they are far too necessary. I am only saying that our judge is our jailer. Be aware that even in truth-telling we are seeking to pick the lock of a cage that opens another one. Koselleck said that in modernity, even the future is historical.

Modernity is not magical. History is humanity's disenchanted answer to the mystery of time itself. We should never lose what is magical about us. Mowaljarlai warned we would become merely what he called 'identity man'. Identity man, this pitiful creature who has no place in the world. Mowaljarlai said 'identity man' left his home shelter for the open Country, his totemic identity remaining locked away, and without it, 'identity man' would 'weaken and wither'.

Let that not be our fate.

This book initially grew out of a series of lectures I delivered in 2025: 'When Words Fail Us: Reclaiming a language of love' (the 2025 Simone Weil Lecture at The Australian Catholic University) and 'Truth Beyond Time' at Federation University.

NOTES

1 Stan Grant, *Murriyang: Song of Time* (Sydney: Bundyi / Simon & Schuster, 2024), p. 218; Albert Camus, 'The Century of Fear (19 November 1946)' in *Camus at Combat: Writing 1944–1947*, edited by Jacqueline Lévi-Valensi, translated by Arthur Goldhammer (Princeton: Princeton University Press, 2006), p. 258.

2 Alice Kaplan, 'Introduction' to Albert Camus, *Algerian Chronicles*, edited by Alice Kaplan, translated by Arthur Goldhammer (Cambridge and London: Belknap Press, 2013), p. 6.

3 Julian Johnson, *After Debussy: Music, Language, and the Margins of Philosophy* (New York: Oxford University Press, 2020), p. 57.

4 Jon Fosse, *A Silent Language*, translated by Damion Searls (London: Fitzcarraldo Editions, 2024) pp. 18 and 20.

5 Simone Weil, *Waiting for God*, translated by Emma Craufurd (New York and London: HarperCollins, 2009), p. 29.

6 Stanley Cavell, *Little Did I Know: Excerpts from Memory* (Stanford: Stanford University Press, 2010), p. 527.

7 See Vladimir Jankélévitch, *Music and the Ineffable*, translated by Carolyn Abbate (Princeton: Princeton University Press, 2003), pp. 48, 120; Vladimir Jankélévitch, *The Paradox of Morality*, translated by Andrew Kelley (New Haven and London: Yale University Press, 2025), p. 227.

8 Søren Kierkegaard, *Practice in Christianity*, edited and translated by Howard V. Hong and Edna H. Hong (Princeton: Princeton University Press, 1991), p. 241.

9 This is an insight both Stan and I have gleaned from Raimond Gaita. See, for example, 'Torture: Can it ever be a lesser evil?' in *Justice and Hope: Essays, Lectures and Other Writings*, edited by Scott Stephens (Carlton: Melbourne University Press, 2024), pp. 343–50.

10 Walt Whitman, 'Leaves of grass' (1855) in *Complete Poetry and Collected Prose*, edited by Justin Kaplan (Washington, D.C.: Library of America, 1982) p. 130.

11 Whitman, 'Democratic vistas' (1871) in *Complete Poetry and Collected Prose*, p. 947.